STUDIES IN ENGLISH LITERATURE No. 12

General Editor

David Daiches

Dean of the School of English and American Studies,
University of Sussex

For my parents

CONRAD: LORD JIM

by

TONY TANNER

Fellow of King's College, Cambridge

BARRON'S EDUCATIONAL SERIES, INC.
WOODBURY, NEW YORK

© TONY TANNER *1963*

First published 1963

Library of Congress Catalogue Card Number: 63-18816

Printed in the United States of America

General Preface

In spite of the now well established academic preference for close criticism of the text of the individual literary work over generalizations about movements and periods, there has been a conspicuous lack of extended critical studies of works other than single lyric poems aimed at the college and university student. The present series is therefore designed to provide studies of individual plays, novels and groups of poems and essays, which are known to be widely studied in the universities. The emphasis is on clarification and evaluation; biographical and historical facts, while they may, of course, be referred to as helpful to an understanding of particular elements in a writer's work, will be subordinated to critical discussion. What kind of work is this? What exactly goes on here? How good is this work, and why? These are the questions which each writer will try to answer.

DAVID DAICHES

Contents

Acknowledgments

The Author wishes to acknowledge the kind permission given by J. M. Dent & Sons Ltd. to quote from Conrad: *Lord Jim*; Secker & Warburg Ltd. to quote from *The Man Without Qualities* by Musil and from André Gide's *Journals*; Charles Scribner's Sons, Ltd., to quote from Henry James's *Prefaces*.

1. Introduction

'Yet can I know how I might react when faced with real danger? Of what simple stuff are they made, the people who can guarantee their reactions at any hour of the day or night! How many soldiers anxiously wait for the event that will prove whether or not they are brave? And he who doesn't react as *he would like to*—whose will alone is brave! . . . The despair of the man who thinks he is a coward because he yielded to a momentary weakness—when he hoped he was courageous (Lord Jim).' (André Gide, *Journals*: 15 Aug. 1914.)

Genre

Lord Jim is the study of a man whose will is valiant and whose behaviour is craven, who is bravely active in his intentions and disastrously passive in his deeds, whose ideal aspirations are courageous and whose real conduct in a crisis is ignoble. He is a man who pursues a glamorous dream at the same time as he flees from an ugly fact. In him the best and the basest of human motives are ominously interwoven. In imagination he is a hero: in actuality he is a coward. He both upholds and betrays those lofty and exacting standards which give life its dignity and society its cohesion. He is both a martyr and a betrayer—a Christ who acts like Judas, a Judas who dies like Christ. He is essentially a simple man but the problems he raises are complex and profound, reaching right down to the roots of conduct. It is this man who stimulated Conrad to one of his major inquiries into the nature of man, the amazing range of his capabilities, and the endless inner and outer threats which he is condemned to confront.

To understand the full significance of the novel it is important to remember the significance of the figure of the hero for so many nineteenth-century romantic thinkers. Nietzsche's Superman and Carlyle's Great Man can be seen as summarising the interest of the century in the hero: the great and lonely individual elevated above the

7

common herd of society by the scope of his imagination, his dedication to dreams and Ideals, his contempt for the prosaic trivia of day-to-day existence. 'In all epochs of the world's history, we shall find the Great Man to have been the indispensable saviour of his epoch;—the lightning, without which the fuel never would have burnt. The History of the World, I said already, was the Biography of Great Men.' With these words Carlyle expresses the whole romantic cult of the unique importance of the supreme individual—supreme by the very intensity of his individualism, his intoxicating sense of personal power and poetic prowess.

The hero may summarise the values and Ideals of the tribe (as in Homer) or he may epitomise various anti-social dreams of revolt (as in much romantic poetry): he is usually celebrated and revered (as in epic and romance) but he may also be challenged and ridiculed (by mock-heroics, satire or irony). Traditional epic shows the heroic values in operation, clarifying and celebrating those qualities which society most admires and aspires to emulate. Romance also tends to celebrate certain Ideals—gallantry or chastity for example—and to ensure that the Ideals pass unchallenged and untarnished, Romance tends to exclude what Yeats called 'the brutality, the ill-breeding, the barbarism of truth', that is, all those un-ideal and anti-idealising elements of reality which threaten the realisation of the Ideal at every turn.

But there is another genre—best represented by *Don Quixote*—which forces the heroic Ideals into damaging collision with unredeemed, earthy empirical reality. This genre does not necessarily utterly destroy the Ideals—Don Quixote is a figure of true pathos with a genuine aura of crumbling and tattered nobility about him—but it challenges their viability in the material world, it shows them up as ridiculous, inoperative, and at times dangerously out of step with the practical needs of a real situation. It may offer a lament for the passing of the heroic Ideals—so that they are seen in a sort of elegiac twilight: but it refuses to take those Ideals at their face value, bringing out their inner weakness as well as revealing their essential inaptness for the external concrete world. This is one of the genres of Irony—not necessarily incompatible with tragedy, but insisting on putting the heroic, the romantic, the Ideal in a sharply realistic perspective. *Lord Jim* belongs to this genre.

Now a recurring figure in this genre is the impostor—the man who pretends or wants or tries to be better than in fact he is. An example of such a figure is the *miles gloriosus*, the traditional bragging soldier who is cowardly in action. Jim is something of a Hotspur in aspiration and he too might have said:

> By heaven, me thinks it were an easie leap
> To plucke bright honor from the pale-fac'd Moone

but in action he has something of the *miles gloriosus* about him and his first 'easy leap' is in fact into a pit of shame. Conrad, that is to say, does not take the hero, the Idealist, at his face value. Jim, *in intention*, is one of Carlyle's Great Men—the lightning, without which the dull fuel of his contemporaries will not burn: the values to which he intends allegiance—courage, self-sacrifice, the personal salvation of a confused society—are the true heroic values, values which Conrad by no means sets out to mock. But Conrad, who was something of a sceptical empiricist by temperament, started to write at a time when western culture was no longer accepting the syndrome of romantic values unquestioningly, when men like Henry James, Proust, and Freud were undertaking a meticulous scrutiny of the complex inward truths of the human heart, when realistic analysis was supplanting romantic incantation as a dominant artistic mood: inevitably Conrad was an ironist, suspicious of Jim's motives, dubious about his redemption, ambivalent in his attitude towards the heroic Ideals. Yet he is never a cynic. Jim's romantic illusions attract him, he sees that they have an importance in determining standards of conduct: but he wants to test the illusions, find out how the hero behaves in a real crisis, see what happens when the glamorous Ideal is immersed in the indifference and hostility of the actual world. And if the heroic Ideals fail—then what do we have left to regulate conduct? This is Conrad's area of interest in this book.

Structure

When first considering a difficult book like *Lord Jim* it is wise to bear in mind a simple but basic distinction—between the actual material of the story (what is supposed to have happened out there in time and space), and the method of presenting this material (the structure and organisation). The material of *Lord Jim* is simply this: a would-be hero deserts what he thinks is a sinking ship; haunted by shame he tries to expiate his cowardice by dedicating himself to the just administration of a native community. He allows himself to be shot by the leader of this community to atone for the treachery of some white pirates whose honourable behaviour he had vouched for. Now this material could be recounted as an uncomplicated sequence of facts by an omniscient author. 'There was once a man called Jim, he did this, then he did that' and so on—but we very soon realise that Conrad's narrative structure has abandoned that simple method whereby author and reader stand comfortably together and look down on a logical chain of events presented in lucid chronological order. Before commenting on Conrad's structure, his shaping of his basic material, I want to quote a passage from Robert Musil's *The Man Without Qualities*. It is part of a meditation by Ulrich, a character who is marvellously aware of most of the major moral and intellectual problems of our age.

'And what occurred to him then was one of those seemingly out-of-the-way and abstract thoughts that so often in his life took on such immediate significance, namely that the law of this life, for which one yearns, overburdened as one is and at the same time dreaming of simplicity, was none other than that of *narrative order*. This is the simple order that consists in one's being able to say: "When that had happened, then this happened." What puts our minds at rest is the simple sequence, the overwhelming variegation of life now represented in, as a mathematician would say, a unidimensional order: the stringing upon one thread of all that has happened in space and time, in short, that notorious "narrative thread" of which it then turns out the thread of life consists. Lucky the man who can say "when", "before" and "after"! . . . What they (i.e. ordinary people) like is the orderly sequence of facts, because it has the look of a necessity, and by means of the impression that their life has a "course" they manage to feel somehow sheltered in the midst of chaos. And now Ulrich observed that he seemed to have lost this elementary narrative element to which private life still holds fast, although in public life everything has now become non-narrative, no longer following a "thread", but spreading out as an infinitely interwoven surface.'

To generalise: when a book has a straight unbroken narrative order it usually means that the author and his readers share a certain confidence about the nature of moral and material reality (Fielding and Jane Austen would be examples). Their perceptions and their judgments work together and are usually clear and sure (they can also, of course, be immensely subtle). Their narrative world is orderly: chaos is elsewhere and unthreatening. But when we find books in which the narrative order has broken up, melted and regrouped into scattered fragments; when we find gaps and leaps in the time sequence; when we find outlines that blur as often as they clear—then we have moved into the modern age, when the author and his public are doubtful about the nature of the moral and material worlds, when the perceptual and judicial faculties do not trust each other, may even contradict each other, when the sense of order is undermined by uncertainty and jarred by recurrent intimations of chaos about us and within us. With Conrad (as with James and Joyce) we first move into that age, and with *Lord Jim* we can say, in Musil's words, the novel 'has now become non-narrative, no longer following a "thread", but spreading out as an infinitely interwoven surface'.

Conrad's dislocated narrative method—'working backwards and forwards' as he called it—is a natural outcome of his belief that though Jim might be simple the whole truth about him and the problems he raises is not: it reflects a conviction that the world is more like a 'damaged kaleidoscope' than an orderly panorama, and that meaning and truth have to be hunted for among the scraps and fragments of experience and then tentatively pieced together like an incomplete jigsaw puzzle. We have moved out of a world of absolute clarity and into a world where moments of fierce visibility alternate with periods of confusing shadow and mist. We have moved into an atmosphere of epistemological scepticism in which the whole Truth can never be known. As Marlow puts it we now move in a world where fullness of utterance has given way to tentative stammerings. 'And besides, the last word is not said,—probably shall never be said. Are not our lives too short for that full utterance which through all our stammerings is of course our only and abiding intention? I have given up expecting those last words. . . .'

It is because of Conrad's doubt—doubt about the finality of our judgments, the adequacy of our perceptions, the completeness of our 'truth'—that his narrative structure is broken, interrupted and re-shuffled. To get at the full significance of Jim, Conrad moves warily and musingly around his accumulated material, listening to many voices, soliciting different opinions, comparing many peripheral ex-periences, juxtaposing segments of past and future so that Time, in this novel, is no longer a linear track on which one thing follows another, but rather an 'interwoven surface' on which things are spread out in a disorderly array which is both confused and significant, random and meaningful. And to achieve these effects Conrad had to abandon his omniscient viewpoint of things and exploit the strategy of the involved narrator.

Marlow

Apart from the first four chapters, all the material of the book comes to us through Marlow, either in his speaking voice as he tells his after-dinner story, or through his letter to a close friend. And the first question to ask is—why have a narrator at all? Henry James has some interesting points to make about this question. In his prefaces he discusses how a writer can extract maximum significance from his material and he often stresses the necessity of choosing a particular kind of spectator. 'By so much as the affair matters *for* some such in-dividual, by so much do we get the best there is of it': he stresses the need for 'a reflecting and colouring medium' and later adds: 'We want it clear, goodness knows, but we also want it thick, and we get the thickness in the human consciousness that entertains and records, that amplifies and interprets it ... prodigies, when they come straight, come with an effect imperilled; they keep all their character, on the other hand, by looming through some other history—the in-dispensable history of somebody's *normal* relation to something.' His point is that it is better to refract the unusual through the normal, to make the alien and remote pass through the near and recognisable, to bring the extraordinary event to us via an ordinary sensibility—because this way you ensure a maximum of mental and emotional involvement. If we were simply told the facts of Jim's life we might feel sorry for him, but as we watched him, haunted, bemused and alone, we would never feel ourselves involved in his predicament.

We would remain disengaged and feel, perhaps a trifle superior, not to say safer. But it is impossible to remain outside the circle of Marlow's auditors. He professes a range of values which are too central, civilised and humane to permit of any disaffiliation on our part. His doubts and questions, his speculations and assertions, his tolerance and self-effacement, the leisurely quest of his memory, the feeling he conveys of being aware yet incapable of the extremes of human behaviour—all these things bring us into the story. We are allowed no certainties, permitted no complacency—we are involved with Marlow, committed to the quality of his mind. And because Marlow feels curiously involved with Jim, the whole problem of Jim's conduct gradually puzzles, implicates and challenges us. We become so caught up in Marlow's hovering interest and delicate probing that when he asserts that Jim was 'one of us'—meaning a western seaman—Jim becomes, by extension, one of 'us', the readers. And when Marlow tells us that 'the mystery of his attitude got hold of me as though he had been an individual in the forefront of his kind, as if the obscure truth involved were momentous enough to affect mankind's conception of itself' we do not back away and contract out of his speculations. For his conviction that Jim 'matters' is contagious and we watch Jim through his eyes, not for vicarious thrills and adventures, but for the generally relevant psychological truths to be revealed.

And what sort of man is Marlow? It is relevant to recall that Marlow made his first appearance as a narrator in *Youth*, a short story written immediately before *Lord Jim*. Here, from the vantage point of age, Marlow recalls his first voyage, a voyage to Bangkok on the *Judea* which caught fire at sea. As he recalls it that voyage was an initiation into the rigours of life at sea, a necessary disillusionment, a salutary realisation that a sense of work is more use than a sense of adventure. In personal terms the voyage meant for Marlow a shift from romanticism to pragmatism. He looks indulgently back at the illusions with which he embarked—'O youth! The strength of it, the faith of it, the imagination of it!'—but he also recalls how he learnt the value of unthinking practical efficiency by watching the older men at work—'There was a completeness in it, something solid like a principle, and masterful like an instinct.' He ridicules himself in retrospect and notes how his hunger for glory was something less than useless in the real crisis. There is indeed a wistfulness, a note of true lament, as he thinks back to 'the romance of illusions': but he has lived to discover that such feelings are 'deceitful', that in the real world they have no chance of survival and that in fact they do not help one to meet the unforeseeable challenges of a savage and unpredictable world. Marlow, we might say, is a Don Quixote who has lived long enough to change into a Sancho Panza, an Idealist turned empiricist, a romanticist turned ironist. In *Lord Jim* it is Jim who is the romantic Idealist and Marlow himself is exclusively the ironist, albeit with a strong sympathy with that very romanticism which he himself has outlived. And it should be stressed that when we say 'ironist' we do not mean a sneering belittler: only a man who insists on regarding things from a realistic point of view. So that by making Marlow recount and discuss Jim's experiences, Conrad makes possible the challenging interplay of two frames of reference, two schemes of values, two sets of attitudes. Marlow is sympathetic enough to do maximum justice to Jim's romantic aspirations, but experienced enough to look at them with the cool eye of the pragmatist. Thus as a narrator he is the man most calculated to understand Jim without taking him at his face value.

Marlow represents the community, the values of the group, yet there is a part of him which is drawn towards the outlaw—'men with soft spots, with hard spots, with hidden plague spots'. He is open to suggestion, 'pervious' to new experience—a quality which draws him almost to the very 'heart of darkness' in the story of that name which Conrad in fact broke off to write while working on *Lord Jim*. For it is in men who have in some way abandoned, contravened, or betrayed the rules and standards of the community that the problems of conduct are most clearly revealed: more so than in the lives of those who are too secure to feel threatened, too well defended to be tested, too insignificant ever to arrive at that point where betrayal and failure are possibilities. Marlow speaks from and for 'the ranks' —but he is more interested in the 'stragglers' and deserters.

Sources

Lord Jim was published as a serial for *Blackwood's Magazine* from

October 1899 to November 1900 and published as book in 1900. For the material of the book Conrad drew, as always, on fragments of personal experience. For instance, while sailing on the *Vidar* he met a Jim Lingard, a white trader who was called Lord Jim on account of his swaggering manner: and Conrad himself had been injured on the *Highland Forest* in 1887 and, like Jim, after a period in hospital he stayed in the East and took a berth out there. But two other sources are more important. In 1880 an old steamer called the *Jeddah* carrying about nine hundred pilgrims from the Dutch Islands left Singapore for Jeddah, the port of Mecca. During some bad weather she was abandoned by her officers (except for one who was forced to stay behind) as part of a scheme to collect the insurance on the boat— which they presumed would founder. It did not sink, and it was towed into Aden just when the captain was reporting the ship lost with all hands. Conrad was often in the East at the time and must have heard about the whole episode. Significantly he changed the motive for desertion from unscrupulous financial greed to a very understandable fear—because fear was, for him, the most basic, the most ineradicable of our feelings. 'Fear always remains. A man may destroy everything within himself, love and hate and belief, and even doubt; but as long as he clings to life he cannot destroy fear: the fear, subtle, indestructible, and terrible, that pervades his being; that tinges his thoughts; that lurks in his heart; that watches on his lips the struggle of his last breath' ('An Outpost of Progress').

For the whole Patusan part of the novel Conrad was considerably indebted, for basic material, to various books about Rajah James Brooke of Sarawak. For full details of this and other sources John Gordon's book *Joseph Conrad—The Making of a Novelist* should be consulted. I will give some summarising quotations.

'After an unsuccessful career in India and England, in 1839 Brooke came to Kuching, the capital of the province of Sarawak on the west coast of Borneo, and helped the governor, Muda Hassim, uncle of the Sultan of Borneo, to put down a local rebellion. In 1841 he was officially created Rajah of Sarawak. The rest of his life he devoted to his new people. . . . Brooke set about improving the chaotic condition of Sarawak according to his ideals. . . . He established peace and prosperity upon a foundation of justice for all so successfully that the population of Kuching grew in five years from fifteen hundred to twelve thousand. The responsibility and the work he took squarely upon himself.' But he did not let the natives down as Jim in effect does, and he did not die a sort of martyr. How Conrad used this figure of romance and constructive energy and his kingdom so far from civilisation, how he related it to the desertion of an old ship, we shall come to later. Now it is worth saying that the second half of the book is an essential completion of the inquiries raised in the first half: it is by no means the weary irrelevance that some critics have claimed.

2. *Lord Jim*

It should be pointed out that this novel differs and deepens with each fresh reading. The first time through one catches hints, echoes and suggestions that remain suspended in the mind because, being uncertain of what has happened, of what is being referred to, one cannot always relate the hints and assimilate the significance of the suggestions. On subsequent readings, knowing the facts, one is more alert to the variety of evidence and opinion that gradually accumulates around Jim. One is not necessarily more positive about one's final judgments, but one is certainly more aware of the rich complexity of the case. Here I shall be working as from a second reading (for some suggestions as to the impact of the first reading see *Conrad the Novelist* by Albert Guerard).

Early failure and eastern refuge (Chapters 1-4)

As well as using his privilege as an omniscient narrator to give us some biographical data on Jim, Conrad in these first four chapters gives us an extraordinary number of hints and some very suggestive 'shots' of Jim which stay in our minds—like held notes in music—when Marlow discusses Jim's crisis and later escapades. The very first paragraph, which seems to be neutrally descriptive in its enumeration of Jim's features and appearance, in retrospect seems to suggest the full compound of strength and weakness in the man—for Conrad is unmatched in his ability to communicate psychological traits through physical details. 'He was an inch, perhaps two, under six feet'—that is, he does not quite reach the traditional height of the hero: he is 'powerfully built, and he advanced straight at you', he is like 'a charging bull'—that is, he is groomed for combat, ready for any crude face-to-face attack, and he prefers a straight uncomplicated approach to life. These are heroic virtues—candour, simplicity, and strength: but we shall see that life does not always allow such a straight track, that there are challenges and dangers too subtle and unpredictable in their onset to allow of the bull's blind rush, that Jim's 'fixed from-under stare' might indicate, as well as determination, a dangerous un-wariness of vision, a too dogged simple-mindedness, a fatal naivety. And we shall see that too often Jim tries to escape inward psycho-logical battles by precipitating an outward physical fight. His com-plaint about the whole *Patna* business is that 'It was not like a fight' but life's problems are not so easily solved and fisticuffs are not always heroic. They might, in some circumstances, be a form of escapism, even of cowardice, since some of our most valiant battles are fought internally, with ourselves. (Cf. Yeats's insight: 'Why should we honour those that die upon the field of battle? A man may show as reckless a courage in entering into the abyss of himself.' That is one abyss that Jim will never attempt.) We are told about his loud voice, his 'dogged self-assertion', which is mainly 'directed . . . at himself'. This hints at his unhealthy self-preoccupation, his excessive concern with his own ego, his lack of interest in other people. When we finally read that he was 'spotlessly neat, apparelled in immaculate white from shoes to hat' we may suspect not only his purity and innocence, his high standards of cleanliness and decorum, but also something of his vanity, his excessive personal fastidiousness, his distaste for the general dirt of the world. (Later Marlow says rather tellingly: 'Men expect one to take into account their fine linen. But I never could get up any enthusiasm about these things . . . all I could see was merely the human being.' Is Jim 'white' all through, or does the clean linen conceal a stain?)

There is a final surprise at the end of the paragraph when we gather that such a striking figure is a mere 'ship-chandler's water-clerk'. An important phrase is then introduced when Conrad tells us that a water clerk 'must have Ability in the abstract and demonstrate it practically'. Jim has 'Ability in the abstract' (the phrase is repeated twice with some ironic effect) but the whole book will go to show that he is unable to employ it when some crucial practical occasion pressingly calls for it.

We are then told that Jim was living behind an incognito and that this incognito 'was not meant to hide a personality but a fact. When the fact broke through the incognito he would leave suddenly the seaport where he happened to be at the time and go to another—generally further East.' 'Fact' is to be a key word in the novel—it represents the challenge Jim can never meet, the threat he seeks to escape: his dreams can never grapple adequately with the factuality of the world. In effect his whole life is summed up in the next sentence. 'He retreated in good order towards the rising sun, and the fact followed him casually but inevitably.' Although it is his 'keen perception of the Intolerable' which drives Jim, there is a deep significance in the direction of his flight. It is not only away from civilisation and the rough western seas—it is also towards the rising sun, a regressive progress, an effort to bury himself in that primordial peace which precedes birth and succeeds death. For the East, in Conrad's work, always carries heavy overtones of that sort of timeless, immobile, sterile peace which we associate with the grave.

Having heard of his flight we are told of his origins, an English parsonage, an abode of 'piety and peace', an area of the world where nothing ever penetrated sufficiently to disturb 'the peace of mind' of a placid population. As Conrad describes it, Jim's home was a sort of idyllic garden, walled-in and secluded behind a 'screen of leaves'. What has driven him away from all that we are to discover: and we may also note that Jim's life turns into a search for another garden, another locale safely walled off from the hazards and challenges of a cruel world. Jim's life is regressive in that, however unconsciously, he searches for, and almost finds, some enchanted place as secure and secluded as his childhood home. From the parsonage to Patusan is a long way—but for Jim they both mean forgetfulness and peace.

Then we are told of Jim's first failure, on the training ship. As a trainee 'he was very smart aloft. . . . His station was in the fore-top, and often from there he looked down, with the contempt of a man destined to shine in the midst of dangers.' Jim is always happiest on the heights, despising the mob below, his eyes fixed on 'the hazy splendour of the sea in the distance' and vague dreams of adventure in his heart. Typically, when he does have to descend to 'the lower deck in the babel of two hundred voices' he escapes into 'light literature', living vicariously 'as a hero in a book'. So that when one day a sudden call to real action shatters his reveries, he is paralysed, unable to make the transition from the world of fancy to the world of fact.

'He stood still'—Conrad twice repeats that phrase which is so full of omen for Jim's future—and while the other boys are dashing around and lowering a rescue boat, Jim feels himself 'whirled around': he staggers as though he finds it difficult to keep his footing in the world of action. At best he can only 'lean over' the side and watch the others automatically doing their duty. In his disappointment he almost feels like leaping overboard to follow them—as an older Jim will feel like swimming back to the *Patna*—because he is in agonies at having lost a chance, not to save others, but to glorify himself. Already his motives seem dubious, already he shows his incapacity for action: and when we hear that to counteract his disappointment he 'brooded apart' and finally despised the triviality of the others' success, priding himself on greater glory to come, we can see signs of his lack of self-knowledge, his habit of skirting personal guilt. He blames the 'brutal tumult of earth and sky for taking him unawares'— not himself for failing to rise to the exigencies of the situation. The end of the chapter places him perfectly: 'unnoticed and apart from the noisy crowd of boys, he exulted with fresh certitude in his avidity for adventure, and in a sense of many-sided courage'. He has no sense of the group, he is alienated from the community, he takes refuge in dreams. When Marlow later asserts that 'we exist only in so far as we hang together' and his friend insists that 'we must fight in the ranks or our lives don't count' we may recall how Jim was from his earliest years—always out of the ranks.

The second chapter describes Jim's early years at sea. His imagination has been disappointed because he finds his sea-life 'strangely barren of adventure' and he can take no satisfaction from mere work, 'the prosaic severity of the daily task that gives bread—but whose only reward is in the perfect love of the work'. He has never been 'tested by those events of the sea that show in the light of day the inner worth of a man, the edge of his temper, the fibre of his stuff'. He has never been exposed to the capricious savagery of the sea, its appalling destructive rage, that terrible 'sinister violence of intention' in the universe which sometimes 'appears on the face of the facts'. Two basic Conradian ideas are introduced here. First, that you can say nothing with certainty about the quality of a man until he has been 'tested' by some extreme set of circumstances, by some event which lays bare 'the secret truth of his pretences': and second, that there is a treacherous streak in existence, a kind of unpredictable malice in nature which threatens sudden annihilation of all that men hold most dear, the kind of malice exemplified by the submerged derelict which lies in wait for the unsuspecting *Patna*, an unseen agent of destruction waiting to disrupt the calm surface of an orderly existence.

Jim, however, has had one slight brush with the 'elemental furies'. His ship went through a week of terrible storms, but Jim, disabled by a falling spar, spent the time in his cabin 'stretched on his back, dazed, battered, hopeless, and tormented as if at the bottom of an abyss of unrest'. Not his fault, certainly, but, 'he felt secretly glad he had not to go on desk'. Where the challenge of necessary action would have awaited him. And after that he is lamed.

The greatest of all tragic heroes, Oedipus, at the height of his powers gave visible evidence of his flaw by his limping and his 'swollen foot' (his name means just that): it is a physical defect which reveals his fatal past. Just so, Jim's laming underlines some basic un- steadiness in his make-up, some ill-footed ill-at-ease-ness in the world, some flaw in his confidence. After the accident he is left behind in the East; Conrad's East—soft, languid, serene and peaceful, and, more significantly for Jim, full of 'suggestions of infinite repose' and 'the gift of dreams'. It is the place where men who dislike 'the home service, with its harder conditions, severer view of duty' tend to stay and go soft, preferring 'to lounge safely through existence' in de- cadent ease. Here Jim goes into a hospital which is high up 'on a hill' —an ideal place for dreaming. And here Jim remains. He renounces the hard active life of the 'home service', succumbs to the dreams and repose of the East, and takes a berth on an old ship with a safe run, the *Patna*.

The first voyage he makes, with the pilgrims, takes place in weather which is hot and calm. The sun 'withered all impulses of strength and energy' while the sea was 'without a ripple, without a wrinkle— viscous, stagnant, dead'. The atmosphere is uncomplicated, unpro- voking, and soothing to a degree which encourages complete self- forgetfulness: it is immobile to the point of death. Jim is content. The third chapter continues the voyage to the moment of the collision. First the impressions of stillness, security, safety and peace are de- veloped: the ship holds to its groove with a steady leisurely con- fidence: the course is so sure that it is drawn on the map by a firm 'straight pencil-line'—perfect for the straight-walking Jim. He has nothing to do but dream (two Malays steer; the importance of this emerges later). In an attitude of somnolent relaxation he conjures up 'imaginary achievements': 'they were the best parts of life, its secret truth, its hidden reality'. Intoxicated by highly coloured dreams of his heroic prowess Jim feels 'there was nothing he could not face'. He dreams best when life is at its softest and safest.

Conrad then introduces Jim's companions, the rest of the white crew: the Captain, an obscene and vile heap of flesh who talks like a sewer and who is to prove for Jim to be 'an incarnation of everything vile and base that lurks in the world we love'; and the two engineers, one a mass of 'soft fleshly curves', the other 'all hollows' and both with dead glazed eyes. These grotesques are examples of the weak and gross human types who are attracted to the enervating East. They are all repugnant to Jim who despises them because they 'did not belong to the world of heroic adventure'. 'He rubbed shoulders with them, but they could not touch him; he shared the air they breathed, but he was different.' But why then is Jim involved with them? In his dreams Jim certainly inhabits a different world: but in a real crisis will he be so untouchable, so obviously distinguishable from these base creatures? Jim does not think about this; he is even rather tolerant of them in a lazy way: but even as he dreams and dozes the crisis is approaching. For suddenly the ship is jarred unexpectedly; they are thrown head- long; an ominous and warning noise breaks the calm 'as if the thunder had growled deep down in the water'; the Malays keep on steering; Jim stiffens in uncomprehending amazement. The Test is on.

The fourth chapter shows Jim in the witness-box of a court of Inquiry, answering questions which are 'aiming at facts'. He is 'elevated'—as usual—but this time it makes him the focus of terrible questions, and curious, accusing eyes. We gather that he is burning with shame, and we see that he is confronted by three judges, all of them 'fiercely distinct'. We should recall that Jim much prefers to focus his dreaming eyes on hazy vague horizons. Conrad makes the whole scene unforgettably distinct, uncomfortably clear—as it is to Jim. Because these judges ignore all Jim's fancies: they are spokesmen for the world of facts. 'They wanted facts. Facts! They demanded facts from him, as if facts could explain anything!' That is Jim's attitude, not Conrad's. It reflects the Idealist's scorn and hatred for the real world which never measures up to the world of dreams, and sometimes seems bent on giving it the lie in the most remorseless manner. These judges only want to hear about those things which are 'visible, tangible, open to the senses, occupying their place in space and time'. They are empiricists. And Jim reacts like the romantic Idealist he is: 'his mind positively flew round and round the seried circle of facts that had surged up all about him to cut him off from the rest of his kind: it was like a creature that, finding itself imprisoned within an enclosure of high stakes, dashes round and round, distracted in the night, trying to find a weak spot, a crevice, a place to scale, some opening through which it may squeeze itself and escape.' Jim is a figure haunted and hemmed in by facts: he is a man desperate to find a way of leaping out of the factual world altogether, of surmounting that enclosure in which he is trapped. He finds a way in Patusan as we shall see. But at this stage all we see is Jim alone and writhing, being forced to answer factual questions 'so much to the point, and so useless', surrounded by stabbing eyes. Looking around the court in desperation he finds a face whose glance is not 'a fascinated stare' but rather 'an act of intelligent volition'. This spectator seems sympathetic, willing to try and understand, aware of Jim's difficulty. Jim returns his glance, and his relationship to Marlow has begun.

The 'Patna' and Jim's first jump (Chapters 5–17)

Having given us this much Conrad the author leaves the book.
He gives us no account of the external details of what happened on
the *Patna*, preferring to let the evasive Jim and the subtle and waver-
ing Marlow involve us in that in their own way. And Marlow soon
lets us know that his attitude to the *Patna* affair is more complex than
that of the Court of Inquiry. He admits that it contains 'a naked fact,
about as naked and ugly as a fact can well be' but he also sees it as
'mysterious', containing something which facts alone will not explain. He first tells of the arrival of the white officers of the *Patna*.
The revolting German captain (described in terms of brilliant carica-
ture) arrives and goes to make his report. The other three wait
outside and Marlow tells us that while he did not 'care a rap about the
behaviour of the other two', the third young man, 'clean-limbed,
clean-faced, firm on his feet' who dissociates himself from the other
two and stands unmoving, staring into the sunshine, immediately
claimed his attention. He looks 'unconcerned and unapproachable'
and Marlow's first reaction is: 'He had no business to look so sound.
I thought to myself—well, if this sort can go wrong like that . . .'
Looking at Jim, Marlow feels he recognises the type. 'I knew his
appearance; he came from the right place; he was one of us.' Out-
wardly Jim seems the ideal representative of certain virtues that
Marlow most admires: 'an unthinking and blessed stiffness before the
outward and inward terrors, before the might of nature, and the
seductive corruption of men—backed by a faith invulnerable to the
strength of facts, to the contagion of example, to the solicitation
of ideas.' Yet Jim, as Marlow already knows, has shown his vul-
nerability on just these three points. And it is this apparent discre-
pancy between appearance and fact in Jim which arouses Marlow's
interest. 'I would have trusted the deck to that youngster on the
strength of a single glance, and gone to sleep with both eyes—and, by
Jove! it wouldn't have been safe. There are depths of horror in that
thought. He looked as genuine as a new sovereign, but there was
some infernal alloy in his metal. How much?' That is a major theme
of the book and it determines the line of Marlow's inquiries—is Jim
gold, or 'nothing more rare than brass'.

The other three men behave very differently from the apparently unmoved and certainly unmoving Jim. The Captain 'burrows' his great bulk into a gharry and 'disappears'—from the face of the known world. Jim is going to find it much harder to 'bury' himself and what he has done. One of the engineers lies wounded and light-headed in hospital, while the other is later found on a garbage heap suffering from D.Ts. He is a piece of human rubbish, in Conrad's severe eyes, and Marlow is not at all interested in him. Yet, on account of Jim, he wants to get to the bottom of the affair. 'Why I longed to go grubbing into the deplorable details of an occurrence which, after all, concerned me no more than as a member of an obscure body of men held together by a community of inglorious toil and by fidelity to a certain standard of conduct, I can't tell.' But in fact he has told us: he represents the values and beliefs of the group, the men of toil. If Jim, who looks like 'one of us', has betrayed those standards which bind the community together, then what is the implication for the men who believe in those standards?

Marlow starts by wanting to discover that Jim was gold after all. 'I see well enough now that I hoped for the impossible—for the laying of what is the most obstinate ghost of man's creation, of the uneasy doubt uprising like a mist, secret and gnawing like a worm, and more chilling than the certitude of death—the doubt of the sovereign power enthroned in a fixed standard of conduct.' What Jim has done represents a threat to those principles which the community need to adhere to if it is to survive. That is the reason Marlow wants to get at 'the fundamental why' and not just 'the superficial how' of the affair. The deep inward truth of Jim is, for Marlow, 'the only truth worth knowing'. And that is a truth which the 'constituted authorities' are unable to ascertain, and are not interested in ascertaining. Mere facts satisfy them, just as mere facts bore and disgust Jim. Marlow must mediate between them, between society and the outlaw, between the empiricists and the Idealist.

But before telling us of his conversations with Jim, Marlow gives us in some detail the life and death of one of the judges—Big Brierly. Brierly is a man who 'had never in his life made a mistake, never had an accident, never a mishap, never a check in his steady rise, and he seemed to be one of those lucky fellows who know nothing of indecision, much less self-mistrust . . . . He had saved lives at sea, had rescued ships in distress . . . his self-satisfaction presented to me and to the world a surface as hard as granite. He committed suicide very soon after.' Marlow hears the details of this utterly unexpected act from Brierly's first mate. Apparently he did everything with his customary care and precision, leaving all the necessary details of the ship's position and course written out in 'neat figures'. He made sure his dog would not follow him and even remembered to take off his gold chronometer, a valued presentation from his underwriters, a symbol of a life-time of duty meticulously performed. Then with no fuss he jumped off his ship. Marlow speculates as to his motives. While listening to Jim's case 'he was probably holding silent inquiry into his own case. The verdict must have been one of unmitigated guilt, and he took the secret of the evidence with him in that leap into the sea.' Certainly Jim's case disturbed Brierly. While it was on he tried to persuade Marlow to get Jim to 'creep twenty feet underground and stay there', he offers him money to run away, he hates Jim for 'eating all that dirt' and calls it cowardice. Most of all he resents the way Jim has betrayed his trust, the white man's standards of 'decency'. 'Such an affair destroys one's confidence' he says to Marlow. Yet why should Brierly have killed himself on account of Jim's shameful conduct?

Conrad believed that all men are brothers, but 'brothers on the lowest side of our intellect and in the instability of our feelings'. A major theme in his work is the possibility of a sudden sense of 'unforeseen partnership' and 'remote kinship' between two people apparently very dissimilar. In such stories as *The Heart of Darkness*, *The Duel*, and pre-eminently in *The Secret Sharer* he explores this possibility that a hidden part of a man committed to order and the rules of society might suddenly embrace and identify itself with a being, a presence, an apparition which seems most antipathetic to his own conscious self, a walking reminder of all that inner darkness and weakness which civilised man has suppressed in order to make group life possible. The stable and reliable Brierly was horrified to recognise a brother in the unstable and unreliable Jim. The concealed coward in him must have given a terrifying start of recognition. So, as Marlow says, 'he committed his reality and his sham together to the keeping of the sea'. He had never been revealed to the eyes of society but he had been revealed to himself and being, like Jim, a man who thinks a great deal of himself, he could not bear to live with the revelation. He buried himself having failed to persuade Jim to disappear and take all his frightful reminders of inner weakness with him. And Marlow is not taken in by this act of self-flight. 'Who can tell what flattering view he had induced himself to take of his own suicide?' Brierly drops out of the book—but the question of the 'reality and sham' of Jim is to linger on, and Marlow is to have doubts about Jim's 'suicide' and the self-flattery that might have accompanied it. Inserting the case of Brierly in the book before we hear the full facts of Jim's case is Conrad's way of complicating our assessment of Jim. For Brierly now remains hovering at the periphery of our minds—a classic reminder of the total unreliability of human appearances, of the sudden crack which can splinter the perfect life.

What brings Marlow and Jim together is a semi-comic incident which vividly shows just how raw Jim's 'exquisite' sensibility is. 'Look at that wretched cur' calls a voice from the crowd outside the courtroom, indicating a dishevelled native dog. Jim swings round, sees Marlow, and accuses him of insulting him. Marlow slowly realises what has happened. 'It was, indeed, a hideous mistake; he had given himself away utterly. I can't give you an idea how shocked I was.' Jim reveals two of his basic characteristics. First he wants to fight Marlow, as a way of dodging his shame: then when he realises his error he apologises, but in a way which deflects all the blame back on to other people. 'You may well forgive me. . . . All these staring people in court seemed such fools that—that it might have been as I supposed.' As when he was the boy left behind on the training ship he has converted his shame into contempt, drowned his guilt in his pride. This psychological manœuvre affords Marlow a 'new view' of Jim. 'I don't pretend I understood him. The views he let me have of himself were like those glimpses through the shifting rents in a thick fog—bits of vivid and vanishing detail, giving no connected idea of the general aspect of the country. They fed one's curiosity without satisfying it; they were no good for purposes of orientation. Upon the whole he was misleading.'

Marlow often recurs to this image, and whether the mist in which

Jim moves is an emanation of his own vague romantic dreams and self-deceptions, or whether it is the mist of doubt about the reliability of human conduct to which Marlow has referred, the effect for the ensuing part of the book is the same. Vivid concrete details—as vivid as only Conrad can make them—alternate with blurred patches which Marlow fills with his tentative speculations. Jim the Idealist is more at home in mists, but Marlow longs always for the clear outline, the sharp profile, the well-defined appearance. Marlow is still left uncertain after Jim's death. 'I ask myself whether his rush had really carried him out of that mist in which he loomed interesting if not very big, with floating outlines' and the crucial chapters 7 to 17 in which Jim and Marlow talk over the *Patna* incident can be seen as presenting an intense struggle between two attitudes towards experience—one pressing for a tough enlightening clarity, the other gravitating towards a glamorous and evasive haze.

The conversation takes place in the dining-room of an hotel and a word must be said about the significance of this setting. Throughout the conversation Marlow often refers to Jim as being 'haunted'. He is in 'hell' as he himself puts it: he is 'in a dispute with an invisible personality, an antagonistic and inseparable partner of his existence—another possessor of his soul': 'He lived surrounded by deceitful ghosts, by austere shades.' Conrad's work is full of people who are haunted—haunted because of some unforgettable act, engaged, like Karain, in 'a struggle against a thought, an idea—against something that cannot be grappled, that never rests—a shadow, a nothing, unconquerable and immortal, that preys upon life.' (The act is usually a betrayal—see in particular *The Lagoon*, *Karain: A Memory*, and *Under Western Eyes*. Compare also Harry in T. S. Eliot's *Family Reunion* who is 'wounded in a war of phantoms' and 'jostled by ghosts'.)

Conrad's austere and pessimistic view of life led him to the conclusion that there were basically two types of people in the world—convicts and idiots. If one was a convict 'one must drag the ball and chain of one's selfhood to the end': that is, due to some insight or some irremediable act, you suddenly become haunted by 'the inseparable being forever at your side—master and slave, victim and executioner—who suffers and causes suffering', i.e. your conscience or your heightened consciousness. Most people, due to the super-ficiality of their lives and the limitations of their minds, remain 'idiots' —respectable but dull, happy but stupid, alive but unaware. These are people who will 'never be called upon to grapple with fate'. It is the convicts—no matter what they have done—who interest Conrad, and we should feel as we watch Jim going through his agony among the tourists of the hotel—there is a convict surrounded by idiots. And when Marlow inserts little details about glasses and crockery, the fatuous conversations of the tourists, the vulgar com-placent comfort of the hotel, these help to throw up in sharp relief the intense interest of Jim, the tremendous reality of what he has been through. As Jim recreates the events of that testing night, the laughter of the other diners seems ridiculously 'innocent and empty', their trivial chatter becomes 'absurd and infinitely remote'. They are un-real. They may travel round the world, but 'the only permanent trace of their improving enterprise' will be the tickets stuck on their cases. They are the 'impermeable' (in Sartre's word): they are in-capable of being touched by life.

The first thing that Marlow notices about Jim is that 'some con-viction of innate blamelessness' keeps checking 'the truth writhing within him' and preventing its full emergence. It is as though he keeps trying 'to save from the fire his idea of what his moral identity should be'. *Should be*: his idealised image of himself fights to suppress the facts of his actual behaviour. He insists that he was not 'ready' for what happened: he was prepared to meet anything 'on the square' but, as Marlow sharply reminds him, 'It is always the unexpected that happens.' He has never shown himself prepared and ready for that and we recall that he was all but asleep when the crash came. He also insists that Marlow 'should not confound him with his partners in—in crime, let us call it. He was not one of them; he was altogether of another sort.' We recall how he had despised them, but we also re-member that, like them, he had abandoned the exacting western seas for a soft job in the East. Just how different he is from those other grotesque types is to become a crucial issue. Marlow brings him back to the facts by saying: 'So that bulkhead held out after all' (it is the first we hear of it), and Jim's reaction is memorable. 'Ah! what a chance missed!'

He is only regretful about 'that missed distinction' and Marlow here makes one of his sharpest points. 'He had no leisure to regret what he had lost, he was so wholly and naturally concerned with what he had failed to obtain.' His mind is fixed only on the *glory* he could have secured for himself: he is not seared by the sense of *honour* irrevocably lost. (He never once shows any concern with the pilgrims as suffering fellow-creatures: he regards them only as a possible source of chaos and panic.) And even while he is talking to Marlow Jim goes off into a day-dream of how heroic he might have been. Marlow deflates him: 'If you had stuck to the ship, you mean!' Jim seems to collapse internally 'as though he had tumbled down from a star'. That is the distance between the Idealist's dreams and the world's facts: it is the distance between the decks of the *Patna* where he should have stayed and that shameful life-boat into which he 'fell'. Watching him go through these extremes Marlow comments —'Ah, he was an imaginative beggar!' It should be stressed that 'imagination' was a faculty of which Conrad was deeply suspicious. In his work it always represents a threat to orderly and efficient conduct because it causes the mind to slide away from 'the saving facts' of life and indulge in immobilising fantasies of terror or glory. Earlier Marlow described Imagination as 'the enemy of men, the father of all terrors': it is also the source of dreams—and neither will help you in a real crisis.

Jim now moves to the events following the crash when they were all convinced that the boat was about to sink. Looking at the pilgrims he saw them as already dead and he imagined the panic if they were all suddenly warned—too few boats, too little time, 'he went through it to the very last harrowing detail'. 'His confounded imagination had evoked for him all the horrors of panic'—consequently he found himself paralysed. 'I thought I might just as well stand where I was and wait'—not frightened so much of death as of 'the emergency', the necessity to act. Marlow understands this: 'I suspect he wanted to die without added terrors, quietly in a sort of peaceful trance.' Marlow knows that pull towards peace, towards giving up, the temptation to quit in a crisis. He understands too that any man would have thought the ship about to sink and that all efforts to help the pilgrims must have seemed hopeless. Jim's appeal to Marlow should make us all uneasy. 'You think me a cur for standing there, but what would you have done? What! You can't tell—nobody can tell.'

But while Jim was standing so still, so entranced, the other white officers were furiously active, trying to lower one shameful boat of flight. They 'had a very clear perception of the actual necessity (and) were tumbling against each other and sweating desperately over that boat business'. Jim, who has the best heroic intentions, was immobilised, turned to stone by his 'faculty of swift and forestalling vision'. He stood apart from the men working at the boat—and did nothing. The others, from the basest motives of pure self-survival, were at least capable of a 'fierce industry'. Jim was 'crippled' in his mind (as he is lame in fact) by thoughts of 'the grasp of the abyss . . . the black end': by contrast the others were 'tugging, pushing, snarling' with mad conspiratorial energy. Jim refused even to look at them, he is careful to insist on that. He stood alone, despising their frantic efforts as so much 'low comedy' unfit for his participation. He stood alone in the doubtful dignity of his 'passive heroism'. When they asked him to help he loftily refused and was called a 'coward'. When a hammer was called for only the engineer had the 'pluck' to go down to the engine room to fetch it. That tool is important. It is wanted for base motives but at least it betokens work and effort, and the getting of it was something beyond Jim's powers as well as beneath his contempt. At least these cynical self-preservers are capable of action. There is a double-edged irony in Jim's insistence that 'he had kept his distance; that there was nothing in common between him and these men—who had the hammer. Nothing whatever.' Marlow comments significantly: 'It is more than probable he thought himself cut off from them by a space that could not be traversed, by an obstacle that could not be overcome, by a chasm without bottom. He was as far as he could get from them—the whole breadth of the ship.'

But between these two apparent extremes—the innocent paralysed dreamer and the corrupt active realists—there was a third type. 'The two Malays had meantime remained holding to the wheel.' Marlow sees this whole group as curiously central and one can see why: the 'actors' in that crucial spectacle represent three distinct worlds of conduct. Jim 'stiffened in the idea of some sort of heroic discretion': the cynical white officers, grotesque in their frantic capers of fear: and the Malay helmsmen who carry on as though nothing had happened. And before going on with the story Marlow inserts his account of the behaviour of the Malays at the trial. When one of them is asked what he thought at the time he is interpreted thus: 'He says he thought nothing.' His explanation is summarised: 'there had been no order; he could not remember an order; why should he leave the helm?' He would not believe that the white men fled through fear because he trusts white men, and proves it by suddenly reciting 'a lot of queer sounding names, names of dead-and-gone skippers, names of forgotten country ships, names of familiar and distorted sound. . . .' The incoherent jabbering of a native—yet it represents that tradition of reliability, efficiency and trust which Jim has betrayed, the honour which he has lost. The Malays simply did what they had always done—thoughtless executants of duty, not imaginative enough to envisage the appalling danger, not base enough or egoistic enough to consider their own safety. These are among Conrad's elect or at least they are the blessed. Blessed with lack of imagination and thought, blessed with an unshakable devotion to the appointed task: too simple to be heroic, too dedicated to go wrong. Having considered them, when Marlow takes us back to that key scene we see Jim in rather a different light. For whatever reasons, out of whatever 'stupidity', the Malays stayed on board—that hard fact has to be dissolved in any sympathetic appraisal of Jim's behaviour. In the curious dream-like calm and quiet of that disastrous moment at sea Jim was obviously open to the solicitation of example. But the example of the Malay helmsmen exerted no influence on him at all. Jim's empty-handed, weak-legged immobility is a very different thing from the unflinching rigidity of the Malays—for they had their hands on the wheel, a location and orientation in the world of facts. Jim, wishing the emergency over and the peace of death already come, preferred to shut his eyes.

The next two things that happened were—without knowing how, Jim found that he had moved, and without knowing why, he found that he had jumped. The other men had finally lowered their boat and were calling for their mate, George, to jump. George in fact was already dead of heart-failure; the pilgrims, to Jim's imaginative eyes, were already a collection of corpses; a storm was coming up; Jim's feet were 'glued to the planks' as he waited for death. All this Jim remembers—but there are crucial lacunae in his memory. He remembers the calls to jump and then goes on: 'I stumbled over his legs.' Marlow points out that 'this was the first I had heard of his having moved at all. . . . Something had started him off at last, but of the exact moment, of the cause that tore him out of his immobility'—of that, Jim can recall nothing. Consciously or unconsciously the motive force behind that first step, a step towards cowardice, is suppressed beyond recall. It is the same with the actual jump. He can remember the horrifying details, but he eludes the moment of decision. Conrad brilliantly depicts his harassed evasiveness.

' "The ship began a slow plunge; the rain swept over her like a broken sea; my cap flew off my head; my breath was driven back into my throat. I heard as if I had been on the top of a tower another wild screech, 'Geo-o-o-orge! Oh, jump!' She was going down, down, head first under me . . ."

'He raised his hand deliberately to his face, and made picking motions with his fingers as though he had been bothered with cobwebs, and afterwards he looked into the open palm for quite half a second before he blurted out—

' "I had jumped . . ." he checked himself, averted his gaze . . . "It seems," he added.'

Jim considers himself 'shamefully tried': Marlow can see that 'he had preserved through it all a strange illusion of passiveness, as though he had not acted but had suffered himself to be handled by the infernal powers who had selected him for the victim of their practical joke'. He even blames the base men in the boat: 'It was their doing as plainly as if they had reached up with a boat-hook and pulled me over.' In refusing to admit any volitional responsibility for his acts, in phrasing everything in passive terms, Jim might be speaking his kind of truth, but he is also warding off 'the grim shadow of self-knowledge'.

And what does the jump signify? In its largest implications it is the fall of man: more specifically it is the romantic Idealist's fall into the base real world, the fall from the star, from the top of the proud tower, the drop from the dream into the lower elements:

for Jim it is the abandonment of the heroic heights, a precipitous tumble from his high conception of himself, from his trust, his honour, from everything which he thought gave glamour and glory to life. Those shouts from the deep darkness urging a completely un-ideal self-preservation must have found an echo in the murmurings from the lowest part of his psyche. Jim thought himself cut off from those cowards 'by a space that could not be traversed'— but by that jump he has traversed that space in an instant, reduced the distance between them to nothing. And as we see him sprawling in that ignoble boat the terrible question arises; has Jim at last found his 'true' level? Is he, at least partially, one of 'them' as well as 'one of us'? In a moment, by a single justifiable leap, Jim's whole set of values has been betrayed, his stance in the world has collapsed, he has aligned himself with the basest of his kind. And worse than that the jump, the fall, the descent goes on forever. 'There was no going back. It was as if I had jumped into an everlasting deep hole. . . .'

Once in the boat with the other cowards Jim's test is continued in a special Conradian manner. For there he goes through the experience of total darkness which for Conrad was the most testing moment of all. 'They saw no lights. All was black . . . there was nothing to see and nothing to hear. Not a glimmer, not a shape, not a sound. . . . The lights were gone.' Jim describes the feeling. 'After the ship's lights had gone, anything might have happened in the boat—anything in the world—and the world no wiser. . . . We were like men walled up in a roomy grave. No concern with anything on earth. Nobody to pass an opinion. Nothing mattered.' Conrad knew that a great deal of our conduct depends on the reassuring sights and sounds of a concrete world and on the presence of other eyes, other voices. The lights of the *Patna*—the lights which would have shown Jim that the ship was not sinking, the lights which would have illuminated the implications of his conduct—they went out. And what they represent are the clues to ethical conduct which the external world gives us, those signs which prompt us to action, irresistible reminders and claims from the world of men. It is when all the lights are out, when the moral eye has nothing to focus on, when the material world is invisible and the human world is blind—it is then that Conrad wants to know how a man behaves, since then he must act according to his deepest inward impulses and not, as is our usual lot, according to a complex of subtle external persuasions. (See *The Shadow Line* for a comparable experience.) Had Jim seen 'the lights' he would have swum back: but due to a shift in the ship's position they were obliterated, and Jim just sat in the boat and contemplated suicide, that ultimate lapse into passivity, a sort of willed evaporation into the indifferent void.

What saves him is the abuse of the others when they find he is not their friend George. 'It was sweet to hear them; it kept me alive.' They snap at him like dirty mongrels and Jim rises to this direct threat. He is always ready for a physical fight. He sits holding the tiller for six hours—solid and ready; enduring though, as always, not acting. Marlow notes the ambiguity of this achievement. 'Firmness of courage or effort of fear? . . . Six hours more or less on the defensive; six hours of alert immobility.' But nothing happened—'a sham from beginning to end'. There is no redeeming action of any kind. Instead Jim watches defensively all night until the other three finally materialise in the dawn light. They sit and stare at him 'like three dirty owls'—another trio of judges, abominable reflections of the dirty part of Jim's own subconscious. They get friendly—'damnably friendly'—and Jim finally shares their water, thus acknowledging some sort of unwilling complicity and participating in a terrible communion with the damned. As the sun rises they all conceal themselves—bury themselves we might say—except Jim, who insists on full exposure to the sun. Significantly he has lost his cap—which can be taken as a symbol of his public identity, his invested authority, his mask. He takes the sun on his bare head all day, perhaps hoping it will scorch out the guilt. Twice more he is to appear bareheaded, and twice more he is to demonstrate his unusual capacity for passive suffering. First at the trial, where all four of them repeat their behaviour in the boat. The three 'dirty owls' quickly bury themselves in one way or another, but Jim insists, perhaps too proudly, that he will 'face it out—alone for myself'. Once again we hear the note of the excessive individualist. It is as though he even wants all the suffering for himself.

All through the talk Jim is trying to bring Marlow on to his side, to force him to identify himself with his dilemma and behaviour, to win from him a gesture of absolution. But Marlow can see that this is a case 'which no solemn deception can palliate'. He sympathises with Jim's innocence and simplicity, the glamour of his illusions, his desperate attempts to salvage his self-image: but he is made aware of 'the subtle unsoundness' of the man. And when Jim insists only on the 'unfairness' of the whole business, and when he speciously pleads that 'there was not the thickness of a sheet of paper between the right and wrong of this affair' Marlow hardens: 'How much more did you want?' The rigours of clarity assert themselves against the delusions of mist.

Marlow next shifts the perspective by recalling his meeting with a French lieutenant who was on board the ship that saved the *Patna* and towed her to port. He is 'a quiet, massive chap', rather untidy, drowsy with wine. He is torpid, stolid, emotionless, and shruggingly inarticulate. He is also scarred and wounded—and we could go to Hemingway to see the significance of this. For Hemingway mutilations represent 'the castigation that everyone receives who goes there long enough'—'there' being the testing arena of action. (*Across the River and Into the Trees.*) This man actually boarded the *Patna* and stayed there for thirty hours, during which time he was only concerned at the lack of wine. But he belittles his behaviour by saying 'One does what one can' (cf. Hemingway's old fisherman who tells himself 'Think of what you can do with what there is'). He incidentally reveals that when he boarded the *Patna* even the cooks were carrying on as though nothing had happened, and, more damningly, he mentions that it finally took only twenty-five minutes to unload the pilgrims from the *Patna*. We should remember that Jim stood still for twenty-seven minutes on that fatal night. Unlike Jim, who claims there is nothing wrong with his heart, this old warrior knows that fear is a permanent inhabitant of the human heart and that 'given a certain set of circumstances, fear is sure to come'. But, he insists, fear is not fatal. 'Habit, necessity, the eye of others'—these help one to remain in control of oneself. Marlow, hoping to get a lenient view of Jim from this 'expert in possession of the facts', points out that Jim had none of those aids at the testing moment. The Frenchman agrees that Jim 'might have had the best dispositions' and that 'one's courage does not come of itself' but he insists that a sense of honour is a real and not a borrowed emotion. His eyes turn to steel and give 'a notion of extreme efficiency' as he delivers these final words, and makes his exit.

' "And what life may be worth when" . . . he got on his feet with a ponderous impetuosity, as a startled ox might scramble up from the grass . . . "when the honour is gone—ah ça! par exemple— I can offer no opinion. I can offer no opinion—because—monsieur —I know nothing of it." '

This immensely impressive pragmatist (like an 'ox', a creature of honest toil, as opposed to Jim, a 'bull', superb-seeming but good only for straight combat), who cannot even remember the name of the *Patna* (because the honourable discharge of duty is simply a life-long habit with him), who has no vainglorious aspirations or pride ('One has done one's possible'), this imperturbable, efficient and impassive member of the 'ranks' has none of Marlow's sympathy and insight into Jim's case: but effectively he passes the most adverse judgment on him, and he speaks as the worthiest possible repre-sentative of the world of 'facts'. His voice, too, must be forever audible when we try to evaluate Jim.

Marlow follows this with a semi-comic recollection about little Bob Stanton—'The same who got drowned afterwards trying to save a lady's-maid in the *Sephora* disaster.' Bob was small and not very strong, the opposite of Jim, yet he died like the hero Jim could only dream of being. A minor note, but it plays its part in the com-plex chord of the book. After these forward-looking interruptions Marlow takes us back to the last day of the trial, the day of judg-ment. The night before, Marlow puts to Jim Brierly's offer of escape-money, but Jim turns it down contemptuously: 'he was eager to go through the ceremony of execution'. Already he is showing signs of that hunger for crucifixion, that rush towards martyrdom which is to end his life. The court duly passes sentence 'in the passionless and definite phraseology a machine would use, if machines could speak'. It is another harsh judgment from the world of facts, a cold sentence of indefinite exile. Jim's certificate, a symbol of honour, efficiency and trustworthiness, is cancelled. Jim leaves the court staggering, unable 'to keep a straight line'—which, as we have noted, is the only way he can really proceed through life.

Then Marlow meets another of those important marginal figures who contribute to and complicate our assessment of Jim. This is Chester, a cynical, unscrupulous pirate; a man of many dubious exploits, immorally undertaken, energetically pursued to a conclusion. He mocks the fact that Jim takes his cancelled certificate to heart. 'What's all the to-do about? A bit of ass's skin. That never yet made a man. You must see things exactly as they are—if you don't, you may just as well give in at once.' He scorns all symbols of honour and takes the lowest, most cynically empirical view of life. He is a Falstaff commenting drily on Jim's Hotspur-like standards. To see things as they are means, for him, to see how things can best be made to contribute to self-enrichment or self-survival. His partner, Robinson, is supposed to have committed cannibalism to keep himself alive but Chester is indifferent to the ethics of the matter: 'the Lord God knows the right and wrong of that story'. In so far as Robinson kept himself alive against heavy odds Chester admires him. 'That's the man for me.' Chester is a man with no morals and no Ideals, but he possesses 'immense energy': the direct opposite of Jim. He asks Marlow to offer Jim a dubious job on a guano island, controlling forty coolies and making them work. Marlow refuses in horror and Chester passes his own kind of memorable verdict on Jim. 'He is no earthly good for anything . . . too much in the clouds.' Or as we might rephrase it—he is no good for any earth-bound activity, he aspires too high. Given his cynical view of reality, Chester can at least see things clearly, he can take hold of the world and use it with confidence and masterful energy. And as he walks away from Marlow with his 'conquering' firm stride we should recall Jim's stumbling exit and become aware of a challenging contrast between the sure-footed cynic and the lame and faltering Idealist. The one is all immoral energy: the other all inefficient dreams.

The three following chapters (15–17) take place in Marlow's hotel room, where Marlow has taken Jim because he had nowhere to withdraw to, nowhere that he could 'be alone with his loneliness'. There Marlow 'stands the stress' of Jim's emotions, lives through his crisis with him. And there even Marlow has a fleeting desire to 'bury' him. 'It would have been so much in accordance with the wisdom of life, which consists in putting out of sight all the reminders of our folly, of our weakness, of our mortality; all that makes against our efficiency': 'efficiency' is a key value word in the book and it is worth noting that even Marlow sees Jim as representing something that threatens it. Marlow sees Jim, fighting for breath, as a figure 'standing on the brink of a vast obscurity, like a lonely figure by the shore of a sombre and hopeless ocean'. That is a simile; it is later to become a reality. But although Marlow hints here that Jim is later to capture 'much honour and an Arcadian happiness' he also tells us that he was never completely reassured by these later impressions and that the most lasting image he has of Jim is when Jim was in his bedroom 'taking, perhaps, too much to heart the mere consequences of his failure'. For now Marlow can see that Jim 'made so much of his disgrace while it is the guilt alone that matters'. In this period of darkness, at the very bottom of the pit, Jim reveals himself in certain key ways. He boasts of his demeanour at the trial—'I carried it off pretty well': he insists that 'I feel as if nothing could ever touch me': he is sure that there will be enough time to 'climb out' of the dark hole of his disgrace: and he cherishes the idea of starting with a 'clean slate'. He is still dodging the guilt, he still feels uncontaminated by the contagion of his base companions of the boat, he still thinks he can have a second chance (as though the *Patna* itself did not constitute a second chance), he is still firmly convinced that he is out of range of the dirty debasing elements of the world, and he has made his exposure and punishment a source of pride. He is keen to regain an opportunity for glory—and oblivious of the honour than can never be regained.

Yet Marlow feels 'responsible' for him. He finds him 'too interesting or too unfortunate to be thrown to the dogs', he feels compelled to guard him from the Chesters of the world. He feels, oddly, that 'should I let him slip away into the darkness I would never forgive myself'. He can detect all the weaknesses and self-deceptions, but Jim is still 'not clear', still in a mist, still not fully accounted for by the facts. 'There were his fine sensibilities, his fine feelings, his fine longings—a sort of sublimated, idealised selfishness.' Marlow still sees him as 'very fine—and very unfortunate' although he also remains 'unenlightened' and full of 'indefinite doubt'. The point is that, for good or bad, Jim had 'reached the secret sensibility of my

egoism': i.e. Jim's very self-concern, his highly individual preoccupation with shame and glory, his terrible outcast state, have elicited a
deep sympathetic response from Marlow's complex and pene-
trable sensibility—as they would not have done, say, from the
French lieutenant. So Marlow feels compelled to help Jim, even
though he is deeply sceptical of Jim's notion that one can obliterate
the past and start again. 'A clean slate, did he say? As if the initial
word of each our destiny were not graven in imperishable characters
upon the face of a rock.' In Marlow's small bedroom with the pur-
ging torrential rain beating down on the roof, Jim has had his dark
night of the soul—yet he seems no nearer to self-knowledge than he
ever was.

The transition between two worlds (Chapters 18-20)

Jim's way of life after the trial is briefly summarised by Marlow
and exemplified by two incidents. Marlow had first sent Jim to a
rich old friend of his who took to Jim's youthful freshness at once
and made him a friend as well as finding him a job. Suddenly with
only the briefest note of farewell, Jim leaves him. He later explains
to Marlow that the second engineer of the *Patna* had turned up to
work in the same mill and had sickened Jim by his assumption of
common complicity. A far-fetched coincidence perhaps—yet Conrad's point is that reminders of a soiled past will be forever turning
up. Jim simply leaves. In leaving he has lost himself a fortune, but
Jim has no interest in money. It is more important to flee from the
pursuing fact. 'This thing must be buried' he says, as though it was
somehow possible to separate the deed from the man who did it.

Similarly in his next job he is successful and popular but when
some old sailors start discussing the *Patna* affair and one of them
maintains that 'It's a disgrace to human natur' ', Jim promptly puts
down his sandwich and beer and tells his boss he is leaving. Egström,
the boss, questions Jim and tries to get the truth out of him and some
common sense into him. 'What is it you're running away from. . . .
You haven't as much sense as a rat. . . . This business ain't going to
sink . . . if you keep up this game you'll very soon find that the
earth ain't big enough to hold you—that's all.' All these remarks go
home: the accusation of flight, the comparison with a dirty animal,

the reminder that a shameful deed will not sink (as the *Patna* would not sink), the chance echo of Chester's insight that Jim has no place on the earth. Jim leaves: but with the superior nod of 'a lord'. He is ashamed but unabashed.

And so Jim goes on, leaving job after job, abandoning career, security, even 'daily bread' whenever the ghost from his past turns up. 'The truth seems to be that it is impossible to lay the ghost of a fact': what puzzles Marlow is 'whether his line of conduct amounted to shirking his ghost or to facing him out.' He strains his 'mental eyesight' but the shades and subtle complexities make it impossible to say whether Jim's behaviour is a form of flight or a mode of combat. But one thing is becoming clear: that Jim, however we assess the motive, is attempting to get away from the world of facts altogether, he is straining somehow to leave the earth. The final futile incident comes when he knocks a drunken Dane out of a bar and into a river because he had made some disparaging remarks. Again he is trying to rebuff a fact by simple physical belligerence: he conceals his shame under his pride and faces his clumsy detractors in a way in which he could never face himself. But this time he is shocked to find that 'everybody in the room seemed to know'. He runs to Marlow—for the second time without his hat: completely exposed, utterly helpless. Marlow of course 'could not think of washing my hands of him' and finds him one more job. But he now realises that Jim is not content with these simple self-effacing tasks. 'He had loved too well to imagine himself a glorious race-horse, and now he was condemned to toil without honour like a costermonger's donkey.' Racehorse rather than donkey, bull rather than ox—Jim has no work sense, and his hunger for glory and glamour is unappeased. He wants an 'opportunity' not just to earn his bread but to satisfy this more urgent appetite. Marlow, wondering what can be done with him, decides to consult his old friend Stein. This man turns out to exist at the real middle of the novel in more ways than one. Stein is not only 'one of the most trustworthy men I had ever known', he is also a 'learned collector' of butterflies and beetles. It is this world-famous expert on insects who is selected to make a central (though not definitive) assessment of Jim. Consider butterflies as beautiful, frail, aspiring creatures soaring above an earth which beetles crudely hug: beetles however are completely at home in the dirt, the mud, the earthy element: they are ugly and repugnant but they have a hard defensive shell and are capable of a dogged persistence in the dense and hampered element of earth which the butterfly could not emulate. Here we have a central metaphor for the extremes of human conduct and values in the book: the frail aspiring Idealist with his glamorous 'markings', and the cynical self-preserving empiricist with his thick skin and foul vigour. Stein's first comment on the rarity of one of the butterflies he is scrutinising contains a warning, melancholy note. 'Only one more speciment like this they have in your *London*, and then—no more.'

But before he presents Jim's case to Stein, Marlow tells us something of Stein's curious life. It is a life which falls into two parts— the first being active and 'adventurous' and the second as strange as 'a dream'. The change came after the tragic loss of his wife. In his active life Stein had been very successful and he describes how he had once been faced by a crisis, an ambush by seven of his enemies. This seemingly irrelevant anecdote is important, for it shows Stein reacting with an instinctive courage and resourcefulness that Jim never had. Stein's reaction to the ambush is more like that of the French lieutenant to the *Patna*. 'I see it all in a minute, and I think— This wants a little management.' His capacity for action is not interfered with by any imagined fears. 'Management'—it is a word to put with 'efficiency' in the value scheme of the book. Stein simply acted, and came through successfully. Yet he was always a butterfly collector, and after succeeding in the ambush he managed to catch the butterfly that he had always dreamed of catching. The imagery here is important. Stein is a romantic—he shows this by his love of butterflies: but being also a brave and capable man of action he takes and 'catches' his romantic opportunities. His dreamed-of acquisition is awarded him—because he is also at home in the real world. Jim, who also dreams but who cannot act, has missed his 'butterfly', has failed to avail himself of his 'romantic' opportunity. The butterfly here becomes the image of all the fine, noble and beautiful things that sensitive men dream of doing, dream of becoming. One can regard Jim as the romantic who failed to grasp his 'butterfly-like' opportunity. One can also see him as a butterfly manqué whose life is

made unbearable by the beetles that constantly cross his path or pol-
lute his air—the four most important being the skipper of the *Patna*,
Chester, Cornelius, and Brown. It is terrible for Jim to meet the
beetles of the world because they horribly remind him that although
he had always thought himself a butterfly, at the most testing moment of his life he identified himself with the beetles. Very subtly
Conrad twice suggests that Jim has something of the beetle about
him. At the beginning of the book Marlow felt that Jim looked too
undisturbed and unmoved and he admits that he waited 'to see
him . . . squirming like an impaled beetle': near the end of the book
in the battle with Sherif Ali in Patusan Jim is nearly 'pinned . . . to
a baulk of timber like one of Stein's beetles' by a native spear.
Simplifying the point we may say—the question is, which box in
Stein's collection of insects does Jim belong to? Does he belong
in the glass cases of butterflies, or should he be relegated to the
'catacombs of beetles'? (It is perhaps worth quoting here an extract
from one of Conrad's letters to Bertrand Russell in which he wrote
that although man has taken to flying—i.e. aiming and aspiring high
—'he doesn't fly like an eagle, he flies like a beetle. And you must
have noticed how ugly, ridiculous and fatuous is the flight of a
beetle.')

Stein, the collector, seems qualified to pronounce on the extremes
of human behaviour: and his verdict on Jim is deceptively simple.
'I understand very well. He is romantic.' Then in cryptic, elliptical,
ambiguous broken phrases he half reveals and half conceals his
philosophy. He sees man as the unstable, unsettled, perhaps even
the unwanted creature of the universe. 'This magnificent butterfly
finds a little heap of dirt and sits still on it; but man he will never
on his heap of mud keep still. . . . He wants to be a saint, and he
wants to be a devil—and every time he shuts his eyes he sees himself
as a very fine fellow—so fine as he can never be . . . In a dream . . .'
(Jim, we recall, closed his eyes in the crisis.) Stein continues: 'And
because you not always can keep your eyes shut there comes the
real trouble—the heart pain—the world pain. I tell you, my friend,
it is not good for you to find you cannot make your dream come
true, for the reason that you not strong enough are, or not clever
enough.' Then he moves on to his famous lines. 'A man that is born

falls into a dream like a man who falls into the sea. If he tries to climb out into the air as inexperienced people endeavour to do, he drowns . . . The way is to the destructive element submit yourself, and with the exertions of your hands and feet in the water make the deep, deep sea keep you up. So if you ask me—how to be?'

But he does not answer this question clearly. Instead he mutters two almost contradictory rules: 'In the destructive element immerse' and 'That was the way. To follow the dream, and again follow the dream—and so—*ewig—usque ad finem* . . .' The connotations around the word 'dream' have spread out in a confused yet bewitching haze. Is 'the dream' life itself, or only man's magnificent but unrealisable aspirations? The world itself, the pile of dirt, is the 'destructive element': man must learn to live in it, but nevertheless he must hold on to his dream. It is deliberately unclear—vaguely, tantalisingly, Stein seems to be trying to synthesise his realism and his romanticism. Typically his comment on Jim is all contradiction, a mixture of two voices, a verdict of divergent values. 'He is romantic. . . . And that is very bad—very bad . . . Very good, too.'

While he is talking Stein takes on a curious stature, an odd remoteness, some indefinable air of the white magician. He becomes something of a Prospero. He seems to be 'out of this concrete and perplexed world' and, like Prospero, preoccupied with 'high charms' and heavenly arts. 'He hovered noiselessly over invisible things' and he seems 'mysteriously busy with immaterial cares'. This is the man, the magician, who is to help Jim.

Marlow can see that Stein himself is extremely romantic and that he puts life in 'a charming and deceptive light' which throws 'the impalpable poesy of its dimness over pitfalls—over graves'. But his vast patient insight into the whole range of humanity gives him a powerful authority. And he puts one very important question to the dubious Marlow. 'What is it that for you and me makes him— exist?' Marlow recalls his reaction. 'At that moment it was difficult to believe in Jim's existence . . . but his imperishable reality came to me with a convincing, with an irresistible force! I saw it vividly, as though in our progress through the lofty silent rooms . . . we had approached nearer to absolute Truth.' The failed, fact-haunted Jim seems to wither away, but what we may call the Platonic Idea of Jim, his 'reality' in another sense, his innate 'truth', emerges from the mystic glooms of Stein's surroundings. It is as though Stein himself were some magic guide between the world of facts, of existence, of the 'destructive element'—and the dream world of pure Ideas (just as in his own life he had travelled from one to the other). At this moment, to Marlow's charmed eyes, Jim, like Jay Gatsby, seems to be true to his 'Platonic conception of himself' (see *The Great Gatsby*). False in fact, he suddenly becomes real in Idea, in all the feelings, aspirations and intentions that he represents. (It is worth noting that in a letter to Sir Sidney Colvin written in 1917 Conrad wrote: 'all my concern has been with the "ideal" value of things, events and people'. But not too much should be forced from this remark.) Marlow leaves Stein among his butterflies promising to do something for Jim, and what Stein does, is, almost literally, make Jim's dreams come true, make the Ideal actual, turn the romantic into the real. He virtually 'creates' or conjures up a romantic realm in which Jim can test his Ideal Truth. He leads Jim from the world of facts into the world of dreams. He sent him to Patusan.

Patusan and Jim's second jump (Chapters 21–35)

Marlow immediately compares Patusan to a 'distant heavenly body' and adds that if Stein had sent Jim 'into a star of the fifth magnitude the change could not have been greater'. This is a new and elevated world for Jim; it is a second star, a second chance. 'He left his earthly failings behind him and that sort of reputation he had, and there was a totally new set of conditions for his imaginative faculty to work on.' At last Jim has escaped from that dirty 'earthy' world of facts and is confronted with conditions obedient to the power of his imagination. Marlow describes the terrain and here Conrad makes marvellous use of the material he gathered from books on James Brooke. There are two hills separated by 'a deep fissure', and the moon rises exactly between these hills, floating 'away above the summits, as if escaping from a yawning grave in gentle triumph'. Now this foreshadows the end when Jim's 'spirit' finally 'rises above the ruins of his existence'. But that moonlight means more than that, as Marlow brings out when he discusses it. 'It is to our sunshine, which—say what you like—is all we have to live by, what the echo is to the sound: misleading and confusing whether the note be mocking or sad. It robs all forms of matter—which, after all, is our domain—of their substance, and gives a sinister reality to shadows alone.' Marlow speaks for the world of hard daylight, of solid matter: but Patusan is lit by the moon which rises above the harsh division of the material world and produces an insubstantial realm of shadows and dreams. And note this: the moon is to the sun what the confusing echo is to the sound. 'Patusan' is, literally, the confusing echo of 'Patna'. Jim has moved out of the world of firm substance, bright light, and clear sound (the world in which he jumped from the *Patna*); and into an unreal world where appearances are subservient to the dreaming imagination (the world of Patusan where he jumps to triumph as he had always dreamed he should). But Marlow, who has no imagination (or so he claims) and is suspicious of all moonlight, is yet to wonder whether Jim's final triumph is not 'misleading', and whether what happened on the *Patna* is not, after all, 'truer' than what happens in Patusan.

Patusan is cut off from the rest of the world by thirty miles of forest. Jim, who can never go back to his real home, has at last found somewhere as safe and remote as the parsonage garden which shielded him as a child. And when Jim appears in Patusan it is, literally, the appearance of his dreams. 'He appeared like a creature not only of another kind but of another essence.' In dazzling white he contrasts superbly with the dirty mud-stained natives, he seems the focal point for all the sunshine, a real god of light. And Jim is delighted with the place because, once there, it will be as if he had 'never existed'. It is the clean slate. He can forget his failures in that other, baser world and live out his dreams without interruption—or so it would seem.

Marlow describes Jim's preparations for departure to Patusan in some detail. Jim is as excited as 'a youngster on the eve of a long holiday with the prospect of delightful scrapes' and he enjoys it all because 'it's like something you read of in books'. He is still trying to live out his cherished fictions, still a child at heart. More significantly his lameness seems very apparent as he 'stumps' around the room boasting of his new prospects. And Marlow is suddenly 'thoroughly sick of him. Why these vapourings?' He dislikes Jim's attitudinising and his persistent sense of there being something left to bury and expiate. It seems too self-important. 'It is you—you, who remember.' The world has other things to think about. And there is one last reminder of Jim's deep distaste for any real action. Marlow offers him a revolver in case of danger. Jim accepts it, but when he leaves he forgets to take the cartridges. For a time he will work miracles with his unloaded gun—but the final crisis will show that there are times when a man must take decisive action, when he must face life fully armed.

The brig-master, Stein's man, who is to take Jim part of the way up river, is another of those Conradian characters who misuse the English language with marvellous suggestiveness. He himself, he says, will never 'ascend' to Patusan—thus hinting at its super-terrestrial location. More tellingly he says that Patusan is 'situated internally'—meaning, of course, in the jungle interior, but giving us the slight notion that Patusan is perhaps some inner world of the imagination. And finally he refers to Jim as being 'already in the similitude of a corpse'. The journey to the interior, then, is to prove fatal. But Jim leaves full of hope, reiterating his old cry that 'I feel as if nothing could touch me' and eagerly looking forward to 'such a magnificent chance'.

Marlow reconstructs the trip: Jim sitting in his dug-out with his 'unloaded revolver' and—a new key image—'his opportunity' which 'sat veiled by his side like an Eastern bride waiting to be uncovered'. And at the first bend of the river 'he lost sight of the sea' which Marlow describes as 'the very image of struggling mankind'. Jim might be 'ascending', but he is also deserting the harsh exacting world of endeavour and toil where most men have to flourish or fail. He is being seduced away from it by a veiled opportunity. He still prefers the glamorous blur to the brutally exact.

Marlow then transmits to us the history of Jim's adventures in Patusan which Jim had described to him on his last visit. Marlow notes that Jim looks on Patusan 'with an owner's eye': he boasts of being needed, trusted, and responsible for the peace and prosperity of the whole place. His work gives him 'the certitude of rehabilitation' and he regards the people with a 'fierce egoism'. But Marlow can see that though he has a possessor's eye it is in fact Jim who is possessed by this land of his dreams. Nevertheless Jim is impressive and has reason to be proud, and Marlow is amazed at his apparent readiness and alertness. Jim then shows him the stockade where the suspicious Rajah had imprisoned him and 'where I leaped over on my third day in Patusan'. He even points out the broken stakes where he made the jump. This, we recall, was the metaphor Conrad used to describe how Jim was trapped by facts at his trial—'imprisoned within an enclosure of high stakes' and unable to find 'a place to scale'. The image has become real—and in this magic world Jim does manage to make a successful leap out of the stockade of facts. His first jump in the other world was a fall, a descent: his second jump is a triumph, an ascent. For in the world of dreams, all insuperable obstacles melt away. 'Good leap, eh?' he boasts to Marlow.

Of Jim's successful battle with Sherif Ali, his control over the Rajah and his rapid, almost effortless, achievement of pre-eminence among Doramin's people, little need be said. These are straight physical events with no problematical gloss: or rather they show the dream smoothly coming true. It is worth pointing out that Jim tells Marlow of his heroic capture of Sherif Ali's hill-top camp (it caved in as only a dream-like fortress of fantasy would) actually standing on the top of that very hill, 'high in the sunshine'. 'He was like a figure set up on a pedestal, to represent in his persistent youth the power, and perhaps the virtues, of races that never grow old. . . .' He has re-achieved the heroic heights—yet is there not just a touch of Peter Pan and Never-Never Land about it all?

Jim has become mythical, almost a god, with supernatural powers ascribed to him and all the glory, applause and worship he ever dreamed of having. To complete his dreams there is his girl; the Jewel which, as with most things he touches, becomes legendary, a rumoured stone of immense value and not the flesh and blood woman he loves. 'Romance had singled Jim out for its own.' But in the middle of his 'charmed life' there is an alien presence—Cornelius, the girl's despicable father. Marlow can assess him just by watching him walk. 'His slow laborious walk resembled the creeping of a repulsive beetle. . . . I suppose he made straight enough for the place where he wanted to get to, but his progress with one shoulder carried forward seemed oblique.' He is an unclean marauder, the stain on the dream. But Jim treats him with careless disdain, with that romantic thoughtlessness or lack of foresight which is once again to prove his undoing. For Cornelius is 'the hateful embodiment of all the annoyances and difficulties he had found in his path'. Earlier in Patusan, Cornelius had threatened Jim with death but Jim had laughed him off with those overconfident words: 'Nothing can touch me.' But the soiled feelers of the 'beetles' are more probing and persistent than he realises. After all, they once dragged him down from his honourable place on the *Patna* into a black hole of shame. Jim is more 'touchable', less out-of-reach of the creatures of the baser elements than he realises. For Jim, with his naive unawareness of hidden evil, is only any good as long as he can 'go straight': but as we can see by watching Cornelius, the beetles are endlessly devious and 'oblique' in their approach. And Cornelius has his own view of Jim which he expounds to Marlow with vile confidence. '*He* save himself. He knows nothing honourable sir—nothing whatever. . . . He throws dust into everybody's eyes; he throws dust into your eyes, honourable sir; but he can't throw dust into my eyes. He is a big fool, honourable sir. . . . He's no more than a little child here—like a little child—a little child.' There is some truth in what Cornelius says (we have seen how 'childish' Jim is): it is Chester's truth, the beetle's truth, the anti-romantic truth seen from the low perspectives of the ditch.

And there are hints that Jim has not quite forgotten or buried his earlier shame. Interestingly, when he catches four natives making an attack on his life he shoots one and makes the three others jump into the river—as though he derived some satisfaction from making them re-enact his first shaming leap. And he himself once says to Marlow that the natives can 'never know the real, real truth' as though he still cannot escape that forgotten world entirely. And he admits that 'the very thought of the world outside is enough to give me a fright'; for that would be to wake from a wonderful dream. So if at times it appears that he has transcended the world of the *Patna*, at other times he seems only to be in hiding from it. He has not quite found utter peace, sheer forgetfulness, pure oblivion and total release from that other world. He sums his state up to Marlow. 'I am satisfied . . . nearly.' Marlow still finds him 'an insoluble mystery'.

Before Marlow leaves Patusan he is questioned earnestly by Jewel, who fears that Jim might be drawn back to the outer world 'beyond the forests'. Marlow reassures her: Jim will never leave her, he is 'true', and no one in that other world wants him. In her anxiety she persists with her questions and drives Marlow to explain why that other world does not want him. In a fury he hurls the answer at her: 'Because he is not good enough.' She recoils from him and runs away, incredulous yet weeping, taking no comfort from Marlow's memorable qualification. 'Nobody, nobody is good enough.' Jim had wanted to be perfect and had fled from all evidence of his defects, chasing his dream. But in Marlow's wiser, more sober eyes, all men are flawed and fallible. Hence the importance of 'the ranks'—'the eye of others'. The bond and solidarity of the ranks encourage men to behave better than they can if they insist on working out their destiny alone.

The difference between Jim and Marlow is brought out at the moment of their farewell. As Marlow leaves Patusan behind him and approaches the sea he feels 'like a man released from bonds' and he revels 'in the different atmosphere that seemed to vibrate with a toil of life'. He is glad to be released from the stagnant dream world and to be going back to his working place 'in the ranks of an insignificant multitude'. Jim does not raise his eyes to the sea: it is no longer his world. When he does look up it is to lose himself in the sunset and to murmur: 'I shall be faithful.' 'Who could tell what forms, what visions, what faces, what forgiveness he could see in the glow of the West!' The magnificent sunset suggests a dazzling glory at the moment of extinction, and a final, eternal repose. Jim's pilgrimage is nearing its end. But to what he will be 'faithful' has yet to be decided.

As Marlow looks back on Patusan he makes the nature of that world very clear. He can recall it as he can recall a painting: 'motionless, with its life arrested, in an unchanging light'. It partakes of that stillness and permanence which is the prerogative of a work of art. All the people there 'exist as if under an enchanter's wand', fixed and revealed forever. The whole thing seems like a creation of Stein's magic wand—Prospero's Ideal, art world. But, says Marlow, Jim himself does not remain defined, unmoving and clear. 'No magician's wand can immobilise him under my eyes. He is one of us.' He is the moving blur on the still canvas, problematically human in a world where everyone else is, as it were, pure essence, sheer Idea (Jewel is pure love, Cornelius is pure malevolence etc.). His ascension, his assumption into the dream world of art is not yet final. His essence is cloudy, too misleading for final pronunciation, too human to be thinned out to a type.

Marlow's last view of Jim is once again an earlier simile come true, for in his anguish in Marlow's hotel bedroom Jim was '*like* a lonely figure by the shore of a sombre and hopeless ocean' (my italics): now he *is* that.

'He was white from head to foot, and remained persistently visible with the strong-hold of the night at his back, the sea at his feet, the opportunity by his side—still veiled. . . . For me that white figure in the stillness of coast and sea seemed to stand at the heart of a vast enigma. The twilight was ebbing fast from the sky above his head, the strip of sand had sunk already under his feet, he himself appeared no bigger than a child—then only a speck, a tiny white speck, that seemed to catch all the light left in a darkened world. . . . And suddenly, I lost him. . . .'

The density of suggestion here is great. Throughout the book Conrad has introduced Manichean hints—the forces of darkness threatening to submerge the principle of light. Jim, all white and luminous, all pure and innocent, here represents all those illusions and glamorous Ideals and aspirations which occasionally redeem life from its darkness, its dirtiness. Yet the darkness is too great for them just as the world is too dirty for them. Jim is here seen being snuffed out. The night has triumphed. But it is not a simple case of the cosmic victimisation of innocence. Jim also appears as the 'child' that Cornelius maintained he was. He can be seen as merely dwindling away from a world he was never strong enough to live in. He is, perhaps, both too good for a benighted world, and also 'not good enough' to resist the encroaching darkness.

Farewell to the butterflies (Chapters 36-45)

With his 'loss' of Jim, Marlow ends his vocal narrative. The last part of the story comes through documents and letters although Marlow's tentative, ever-uncertain, ordering of the material is still in evidence. His letter is to that friend who 'maintained that we must fight in the ranks or our lives don't count'. Marlow, that is, has entrusted Jim's case to a man like himself only more severe in his judgments. It is to this man that Marlow points out Jim's arrant individualism—'Jim had no dealings but with himself'—and puts the question of 'whether at last he had not confessed to a faith mightier than the laws of order and progress'. This last section of the book is the final inquiry into Jim's 'truth', his 'faithfulness', his 'reality', the law and logic of his life.

First comes an enclosed note from Jim in 'a commonplace hand' (writing often reveals character in Conrad—Marlow's writing is 'upright and angular'): it is merely an inarticulate and unfinished cry. 'An awful thing has happened. . . . I must now at once . . .' At once do what? Complete his redemption or confess his failure? Jim does not say. Then comes an old letter from Jim's father written just before the *Patna* affair and apparently carefully preserved by Jim. It includes a warning uttered from his father's complacent and untroubled corner of the universe: 'who once gives way to temptation, in the very instant hazards his total depravity and everlasting ruin. Therefore resolve fixedly never, through any possible motives, to do anything which you believe to be wrong.' This inflexible unimaginative morality is not only too harsh to live by (only the untested could have framed it): it leads to a dangerous preoccupation with self, with one's own motives, instead of encouraging one to regard the claims and exigencies of the external situation. We can see the source of Jim's excessive self-concern and egoism. It is a typical Protestant trait.

Marlow then recounts his final visit to Stein after Jim's death. There he gets some important hints. Tamb' Itam, Jim's devoted native bodyguard, merely says: 'He would not fight.' We recall those unloaded revolvers and Jim's incorrigible distaste for action. Then Jewel, cold and crystalline in her grief, says: 'He has left me . . . you always leave us—for your own ends. . . . He fled as if driven by some accursed thing he had heard or seen in his sleep.' She further insists that 'he had been driven away from her by a dream', and that he was 'false'. Here Stein breaks in and desperately asserts the contrary: 'No! No! Not false! True! true! true!' The crucial unresolved question is left in the air. Did Jim finally catch his dream, or did he rather complete his flight from an old ghost? Was he finally false or true?

Marlow ends his letter and we go on to his reconstruction of what happened between Brown and Jim. Brown is a major figure: the most important beetle in the book. Lawless, arrogant, energetic, a man who has devoted himself to a satanic life of pure destructiveness: his only fear is of 'imprisonment' for he is too much the man of action to endure 'the bare possibility of being locked up'. His dominant emotion is 'the lust of battle': his greatest pleasure is to 'play havoc' with anything in the world that opposes him. It is this man who, in desperation for food and water, stumbles into Patusan, that harmonious realm where Jim has raised order out of jungle chaos. Aided by that fellow-beetle Cornelius, Brown starts to see Patusan in terms of possible 'loot'. He has the possessor's eye as well as Jim but instead of seeing Patusan as a moral mission, an opportunity for benevolent constructive impulses, he sees it as mere spoil, something 'to tear to pieces, squeeze, and throw away'. He wants to turn Jim's kingdom into a ruin, to see it running in blood. He has an Iago streak in him, the diabolical compulsion to bring everything to chaos, to reduce fine things to a mess, to 'unpeg' the harmonious exalted music of the naive and noble Othellos of the world. This is the man who turns up to confront Jim.

With his dying breath Brown reveals to Marlow how instinctively he hated Jim. 'He a man! Hell! He was a hollow sham. As if he couldn't have said straight out, "Hands off my plunder!" blast him! That would have been like a man! Rot his superior soul! He had me there—but he hadn't devil enough in him to make an end of me. . . . Fraud!' Marlow thus reimagines the scene when Jim and Brown finally met. 'I know that Brown hated Jim at first sight.' Hated him for his youth, his neat white clothes, his 'don't you touch me' airs, his superior distaste for action, his lack of 'devil'. All these things revolt the man of dirty devilish energy. They met on the hill where Jim had effected his second 'leap'—'into the trust, the love, the confidence of the people'—and they stood, says Marlow, 'on the opposite poles of that conception of life which includes all mankind'. A real threat has burst into Jim's dream world: the challenge to 'act' in face of a real menace is on him again.

But Brown's terrible rhetoric, full of satanic insights and damaging thrusts, paralyses Jim. Brown is indeed the anti-heroic, anti-romantic, anti-Idealist supreme. And he is supremely successful because he has an uncanny instinct for fingering—'touching'—all the soft spots in Jim's armour of Idealism. Thus he admits that he was driven to Patusan by hunger and asks why Jim is 'skulking' there. He asks for a fight or a clear road, admitting that he is in a tight corner.

'And I would let you shoot me, and welcome. . . . But it would be too easy. There are my men in the same boat—and, by God, I am not the sort to jump out of trouble and leave them in a d—d lurch.' After this wounding blow and this contempt for suicide as the 'easy' way out (it is to be Jim's way), Brown drives his point home. 'I've lived —and so did you though you talk as if you were one of those people that should have wings so as to go about without touching the dirty earth. Well—it is dirty. I haven't got any wings.' This is the beetle's contempt for all those men who try to live like butterflies; the man without wings yearning to drag down into his element all those superior beings who think they can live without touching the earth; the creature of dirt longing to soil the immaculate disdain of the young man in white. Brown's final thrust reduces Jim to complete impotence for he says he is sure that Jim will understand that 'when it came to saving one's life in the dark, one didn't care who else went —three, thirty, three hundred people'. Brown at least has a sort of honesty, a courage of his immoral convictions which Jim has never had. It is a base and murderous integrity—but it is a source of strength. Brown also threatens to give Jim at least some sort of trouble if he does not escape, pointing out that 'even a trapped rat can give a bite'. Jim's quick answer reveals once again his incurable hatred for any vital involving action with the low creatures of the world. 'Not if you don't go near the trap till the rat is dead.' He wants to stand right back from Brown, the more so because 'there ran through the rough talk a vein of subtle reference to their common blood, an assumption of common experience; a sickening suggestion of common guilt, of secret knowledge that was like a bond of their minds and of their hearts'.

Here is an 'unforeseen partnership' indeed. Jim cannot bear to be reminded of the beetle-like elements in his own character that lurk under the butterfly markings. He takes the easy way out and promises Brown a clear road and a safe passage: a dangerous thing to promise a man of such revealed and avowed treachery, but Jim refuses to join combat with his ghost. For Brown is no chance opposition, not a mere reminder that a bad penny always turns up. He is an 'emissary' from the factual world 'pursuing' Jim to 'his retreat', living evidence of the horrible contagion of reality. (A comparable situation occurs in *Victory*—a book which should be studied with *Lord Jim*.) Brown is all that menace and danger which no man can avoid: he represents the inescapability of the beetle types of the world, the far-reaching contaminating persistence of their immoral ferocity and murderous truth. More subtly he reminds Jim, he reminds us, that every man alive has something of the beetle element in him. The threat is not wholly external for, as Marlow remarks after Brown has perpetrated his ugly massacre, his behaviour was 'a demonstration of some obscure and awful attribute of our nature which, I am afraid, is not so very far under the surface as we like to think'. The beetles are not only all about us, they are deep within us.

So Jim backs out of the fight: he even refuses to lead the party that is to see Brown properly out of the area. Brown, acting on the suggestion and with the help of Cornelius, attacks that party from behind before escaping, and Dain Waris, the son of Doramin, is killed. Jim's reputation, his whole achievement, is shattered. Faced with a real threat he has failed—failed to fight, failed to live up to his responsibility to the native people, failed to act. His motives for non-violence may seem admirably humane, but the results are disastrous. His ruined kingdom turns against him.

Yet in a sense this gives him the chance he has been waiting for all his life. He had promised to 'answer with his life for any harm' that should come to the natives, just as in the war with Sherif Ali he had 'made himself responsible for success on his own head'. Now he can become a martyr, take the evil acts of others on his own head: he can die with dignity and glamour to vindicate his honour. He can—as he always could—take his punishment *passively*: he can exult on the cross. He can see this as a way of proving his power by conquering his 'fatal destiny'. The world is at fault. He will transcend it. So, hatless for the third time, he goes to Doramin knowing that the chief must shoot him for vengeance. 'He hath taken it upon his own head' says a voice, and he turns: 'yes. Upon my head.' He faces Doramin: 'I am come ready and unarmed.' And that is his last word before Doramin shoots him. Proud, unflinching, honourable—*unarmed*. It is his epitaph. For he was always unequipped to take strenuous issue with a fierce and hostile world.

He dies to vindicate a superior Ideal. Seen in this light Marlow can talk of 'the sheer truthfulness of his last three years of life'. To the end, Jim was faithful to his dream, true to his Ideal. But there is another view of the matter. His martyrdom is also a suicide, for he refuses to fight and escape from the angry natives as Tamb' Itam and Jewel urge him to do. His death is an easy way out. It is the final relapse into peace, the merciful release from the world of action. It is the end of his flight from a ghost, the last shutting of eyes that never again need be reopened, an escape into an immobility which can never be disturbed. Jim has been true to his weaknesses as well. Now, at last, he can indeed never be 'touched'. He has jumped out of a life which he found too foul, too strenuous, too challenging. (One could even say that Jim was 'seduced' into death by his 'veiled opportunity': the connection between romanticism and the death-wish was noted by Thomas Mann who wrote: 'Romanticism bears in its heart the germ of morbidity, as the rose bears the worm; its innermost character is seduction, seduction to death.') Whether this last jump was a final ascent into triumph or another descent into shame, a consummation or an evasion, Marlow will never be sure.

But either way he was 'egoistic' to the end. For like his jump from the *Patna*, his final jump out of life also involved a betrayal, an abandonment. For once again he leaves someone behind. He left 'a living woman to celebrate his pitiless wedding with a shadowy ideal of conduct'. He left Jewel to embrace his veiled exotic 'opportunity', his Eastern dream. Having once failed in his public duty he has now disregarded his private obligations. His 'exalted egoism' has, as before, made him oblivious to the claims and needs of other people. His allegiance was always to the Abstract, the Ideal: he was never equal to the demands of the actual. Marlow ends his account on a note of doubt. 'Is he satisfied—quite, now, I wonder?' Jim is left in those ambiguous, ambivalent mists from which Marlow was always trying to extract him. Was he false or true, too good or not good enough for this world? If he was 'faithful' to his Ideal, then what of his conduct in the world of men: if he betrayed the claims of the real world, then was it the fault of external conspiracy and malevolence, or did the flaw lie deep within him? Was he a butterfly with broken wings—or was there a stain of the beetle concealed amongst those glamorous, beautifully coloured markings? Final judgment is something Conrad systematically dissuades us from passing. But we can say this. No matter how admirable and necessary and touching the illusions and dreams of the romantic Idealist are, they reveal themselves as a fatal drawback in the world of action. They tend to produce immobility, inaction, closed eyes, and a dangerous longing for passivity and peace, when a skilled management of the palpable facts of some concrete crisis is called for. They may lead to a glorious martyrdom but they will not produce efficiency: and Conrad was unsentimental enough to know that it is sometimes easier to die than to work. No matter how fine and sympathetic his dreams are, the self-preoccupied Idealist is out of place in a world which cries out for pragmatists who can 'work in the ranks'. Perhaps Jim's spirit did 'rise above the ruins of his existence', perhaps he was 'constant' to some superior Idea of conduct, perhaps his final gesture was a 'victory'. Perhaps he was too fine for the beetle-ridden muck heap of the world. But no matter how base 'the destructive element' is, the world is the world and man must learn to live in it—seeking only such honour as is consistent with an unremitting efficiency. Jim cannot live in the world: he can only triumph in dream, and reality will not let him dream for very long. The end of the novel can be seen as a reluctant valediction, a farewell to the butterflies and the men like them who are too fine, too frail and, perhaps, too flawed to grapple with existence.

'Stein has aged greatly of late. He feels it himself, and says often that he is "preparing to leave all this; preparing to leave . . ." while he waves his hand sadly at his butterflies.'

3. Conrad's World: The Complacent, the Efficient and the Damned

'Man is amazing, but he is not a masterpiece' (Stein in *Lord Jim*). Every great writer has a vision; he creates a recognisable universe which contains selected raw material from the real world, intensified and transformed into art by the very power of that vision. He gives us reality saturated with insight, experience exposed by the passion of his own perspective. He does not bully us with a creed (that is for the preacher); rather he opens up unsettling areas of existence and shows us values in the making, and in the destroying. I can only simplify Conrad's world, and any such summary is a falsification. But a few points can help us to focus on what most preoccupied him and compelled him to utterance.

Writing of his own sudden departure from Poland, Conrad made three interesting points about that curious break of continuity in his life. He found his impulses quite 'mysterious': he described his act as 'taking a standing jump out of his racial surroundings and associations': and looking back on his subsequent life he regarded it as 'a series of betrayals'. I am not seeking for autobiographical precedents, but it is interesting to note that Conrad had a personal interest in three of the problems which provide major themes in his work. He was always interested in those sudden impulsive actions which break the continuity of a safe established way of life, those momentary perhaps irrational deeds which irrevocably mark a man and commit him to a way of life utterly different from the lives of those who have never strayed or fallen or 'jumped' in every sense of the word. For the complacent upholder of civic virtue who rejects the idea that he might ever deviate from the prescribed grooves of conduct, Conrad had a barely controlled contempt. 'They walk the road of life, the road fenced in by their tastes, prejudices, disdains or enthusiasms, generally honest, invariably stupid, and are proud of never losing their way.' Such men have been 'disdained by destiny'. But there are a few men who without planning or intending it, are forced into a damning act, or decision, by a completely unforeseen configuration of circumstances, by some extreme and unpredictable menace, some unavoidable exposure to a hostile and undermining situation. And this act constitutes a sudden and final departure from the known edifices of convention. There are, that is to say, some men who 'jump' —who fall into the abyss. And the jump usually turns out to be irremediable. Conrad's work is full of people who 'jump' or who do something which he describes by metaphors of fall and descent: e.g. Almayer, Willems, Kurtz, Captain Whalley, Jim, Razumov, Heyst etc. They face different predicaments, are subject to different weaknesses, act and take decisions of different gravity: their deaths mean different things to each of them. But under one sort of duress or another they all take a plunge out of a rigidly conventionalised and ordered way of life. It is in these people that Conrad thought we could see the moral problems of the world working themselves out. For these men enter the moral universe. By their irrevocable acts they make themselves significant, they involve themselves in an irreversible journey down into the deep truths of the human heart. And as they toil and writhe and squirm in their anguish, rage or remorse, they lose that dull, doughy opacity which most human lives have, and become transparent so that in them we can watch some profound human truths being worked out. In their persons the inner problems of conduct and conscience are unpeeled and exposed. And usually this fatal jump is an act of betrayal, that most offensive of all acts which alienates a man from his fellows and isolates him with the remorseless ghosts of his past. Conrad believed in the value of the ranks, of routine, of orderliness and commitment to certain simple pragmatic standards of conduct—precisely because he had such a profound sense of everything in life which challenges and undermines them. He vividly communicates the necessity for simple decency of conduct only because he has a telling vision of the external and internal chaos which threatens that decency and drives men out and away from the solidarity of the ranks.

That is why Jim's case 'matters' so much to Marlow, for Jim has demonstrated the terrible divorce between intention and action, the weakness inherent in our most cherished ideals. He is our best dreams and our worst vulnerabilities. 'He appealed to all sides at once—to the side turned perpetually to the light of day, and to that side of us which . . . exists stealthily in perpetual darkness.' Jim is not a simple criminal, for then he would not matter. The criminal consciously opts to work against society, in cynical disregard of the rules of the ranks. Jim has been found out 'not in a crime but in a more than criminal weakness'. This is the central focus in Conrad's vision of man—not his conscious evil but his unwilling fallibility: 'it is from weakness unknown, but perhaps suspected, as in some parts of the world you suspect a deadly snake in every bush—from weakness that may lie hidden, watched or unwatched, prayed against or manfully scorned, repressed or maybe ignored more than half a lifetime, not one of us is safe.' Is it because of this malingering weakness in man that Conrad was suspicious of ideas and the imagination: for these activities corrode those crude confidences and certitudes which enable the majority of mankind to keep a grip on their lives, they lead to 'perversions of the nerves'. Thus Conrad's ideal figure is not the intellectual or the imaginative romantic Idealist, not—certainly—the complacent bourgeois who never exposes himself to the rigours of the universe, but men like the French lieutenant who know fear but hold on to efficiency, and those Malay natives who keep on steering in blessed simplicity and who are imperturbable because they are unconscious. (See also the figure of Captain Singleton in *Nigger of the Narcissus*.) Steering is important to Conrad—but not in the same way as it was to Shaw when he made his Don Juan say: 'To be in hell is to drift: to be in heaven is to steer.' For Shaw, a social meliorist and optimist, meant that men and society should allow themselves to be guided by their intelligence so that they can hurry up and arrive at their final happy destination, a Utopia on earth. Conrad saw no such destination, and suspected the mind as a disrupter of proper conduct. He was pessimistic about the ungovernable hostilities of nature and the inexpugnable weaknesses in man. Steering meant only keeping your hands firmly round the palpable facts, fixing your eye on the immediate task. It was not a way of getting to heaven—only an indispensable strategy for keeping chaos at bay. If Jim had had his hands on a wheel it might have anchored him to his duty: but then he would not have been a dreamer, he would not have jumped, he would not have been harried by ghosts and seduced by opportunities. He would not have engaged Conrad so profoundly—and we would have been without one of the greatest studies of conduct in our literature.

A Short Bibliography

The most useful Conrad criticism seems to me to be contained in the following works:

John Gordon, *Joseph Conrad—The Making of a Novelist*
Albert Guerard, *Conrad the Novelist*
Thomas Moser, *Joseph Conrad: Achievement and Decline*

For some valuable general remarks on Conrad see:

Morton Dauwen Zabel, *Craft and Character in Modern Fiction*
F. R. Leavis, *The Great Tradition*

For some illuminating suggestions about the origin and tradition of the impostor, *miles gloriosus*, figure, see:

Northrop Frye, *Anatomy of Criticism*

The best biography of Conrad is:

Jocelyn Baines, *Joseph Conrad*

Other useful works include:

D. Hewitt, *Conrad: A Reassessment*
M. Bradbrook, *England's Polish Genius*

Other works by Conrad which will enrich a study of *Lord Jim* are:

Youth, The Heart of Darkness, Under Western Eyes, and *Victory*

Other works by Conrad mentioned in the text:

An Outpost of Progress, The Duel, The Secret Sharer, Lagoon, Karain: A Memory, The Nigger of the Narcissus, and *The Shadow Line*

Index